the *BLACKJACK*

BLUEBOOK

the Right Stuff for the Serious Player

FRED RENZEY

、 **BLACKJACK BLUEBOOK**
the "right stuff" for the serious player

Copyright © 1996 by Fred Renzey

CHICAGO SPECTRUM PRESS

^C/o Blackjack Bluebook
P.O. box 598, Elk Grove Village, IL. 60009
phone (847) 228-9922

SECOND PRINTING
1998

Printed in Canada

The material contained in this book is intended to educate and inform the reader. It is further cautioned that gambling is an uncertain venture carrying a broad range of financial consequences.

ii

THIS BOOK IN A NUTSHELL

The average casino gambler out there should be able to find a blackjack book that finally tells it like it is. That means no promises of easy money or other delusions of grandeur; just the cold hard facts about the most popular table game on the casino floor.

That straight-line, realistic approach may or may not sell this book, but it *will* tell you what your chances *are,* what they *are not* and what they *can be* at casino blackjack.

With the right information and the properly honed skills, you do have a chance to win and remain a winner. Without them, you've got *no shot!* Inside, you'll learn that;

A) Blackjack has two characteristics which make it a game of skill that is difficult but possible to beat.

B) By learning to play your hands correctly, you can reduce the casino's advantage over you to roughly a 100 to 99 proposition.

C) By keeping track of the cards, the player can actually gain the upper hand in the game.

D) Playing well enough to win at blackjack takes more dedication than most people are willing to devote.

E) The edge an expert player can gain is very small and is subject to counter-tactics from the other side of the table, making winning even more difficult.

F) Among casino-banked table games, blackjack still offers the good player his best chance to win at casino gambling.

iii

ACKNOWLEDGMENTS

Cover photo by Emil Schiavo

Cover design by Dorothy Kavka

Computer data by Stanford Wong's
"Blackjack Count Analyzer"

Proof reading by Emily Mendoza and Stan Weiss

TABLE of CONTENTS

Blackjack Quiz... 3

SECTION "A": Unique Nature of Blackjack.......... 11

Chapter 1: Why Blackjack................................. 12
Basic Principle of Profitable Gambling.................... 13

Chapter 2: The House Edge............................... 19
Who has the Advantage.. 20
Maximizing Player Options.................................... 21

Chapter 3: Rules of the Game........................... 24
Dealer's Soft 17... 26
Hitting, Standing, Doubling Down........................... 27
Splitting Pairs... 28
Insurance... 29
Surrender... 32

SECTION "B": What Makes Gambling Tick?....... 34

Chapter 4: Blackjack Myths............................... 35
"I'm Due to Win".. 36
"Quit when You're Ahead"..................................... 38
"The Order of the Cards is Sacred".......................... 43
"Bad Players at the Table Hurt You"......................... 46
"Betting Progressions can Beat the House"................... 50

SECTION "C": Proper Blackjack Strategy........... 60

Chapter 5: The Basic Strategy........................... 61
Blackjack's Primary Fundamentals........................... 63
The Complete Basic Strategy................................ 66
Dealer's Bust-out Rate...................................... 71
Commonly Misplayed Hands.................................... 72
Insuring a Blackjack.. 75
Bad Soft Doubles.. 78
The Rule of "9"... 80
Insure a Good Hand?... 82
Insurance for Basic Strategy................................ 83
Rule Variations and their Percentages...................... 86
Doubling for Less... 88
Player's Hand Odds.. 90

Chapter 6: Borderline Blackjack hands.............. 93

Composition-Sensitive Hands.................................. 95
Board-Sensitive Hands... 97
Light Board / Heavy Board....................................... 100

Chapter 7: The High Card / Low Card Axiom....... 108

Spanish "21", Pinochle Blackjack............................. 110

SECTION "D": Keeping Track of the Cards......... 115

Chapter 8: The Key Card Count............................ 116

How Much is my Wallet Worth?"............................. 117
The Counting Process.. 119
Betting Strategy.. 123
Playing the Advantage Strategy............................... 125
The Complete Key Card Count Strategy.................. 128

Chapter 9: The Black Ace Count........................... 131

The Complete Black Ace Count Strategy................. 133
Up-Grading the Black Ace Count............................. 135
The Up-Graded Black Ace Count Strategy............... 136

Chapter 10: The Art and Science of Skillful Play. 139

Playable Rules.. 140
Deck Penetration... 141
Number of Players... 143
Betting Spread.. 146
Table Hopping.. 149
Playing 2 Hands at the Same Time.......................... 150
The Right Time to Quit.. 152
Bankrolling... 153
Table Image.. 154
Maintaining Poise... 156

Chapter 11: The Mentor Count.............................. 160

Testing Various Count Systems............................... 162
The Mentor Card Count... 166
A "100" Counting Base.. 168
The True Count.. 169
Variable Playing Strategy Index Charts.................... 176
The Value of a Variable Playing Strategy................. 181

Recommended Reading..................................... 184

WHAT'S YOUR BLACKJACK I. Q.?

So you like to play casino blackjack. Think you know the game pretty well? Of course you do. I've never met a blackjack player who figured he was a bad one. If you ever need advice on how to play a blackjack hand when you're at the table, just ask the player to the left of you; or to your right. They always seem to have the answers. But do they really?

Following is a twelve question "I. Q." test for the game of casino blackjack. It's multiple choice. It doesn't just quiz you on the basic strategy. If it did, you could get a perfect score on it by simply memorizing a chart. But would that mean you really know the game? Not necessarily. There is a lot to be aware of at the blackjack table besides your basic hitting, standing and doubling down.

Go ahead, take the quiz. I think you'll find it both interesting and educational. It starts out with some very simple basics and progresses on from there. The answers are provided at the end along with detailed explanations and scoring. You may find that you don't know as much about casino "21" as you thought. In that case, go ahead and read the rest of this book. It will probably make you a much better blackjack player.

3

Blackjack Quiz

1) A "stiff" is:
a) a player who won't pay off his marker.
b) when you catch a deuce on your double down.
c) a hard total between 12 and 16.

2) Third base is:
a) the seat just next to the dealer's shoe.
b) the third player to act in the hand.
c) the seat just next to the discard tray.

3) A "soft" hand is:
a) a hand containing an Ace counted as 11.
b) a hand containing an Ace counted as 1.
c) a hand with a total of 11 or less.

4) The most important card in the game of black-jack is:
a) the deuce
b) any 10-count card
c) the five
d) the Ace

5) Which of these hands is it most important that you hit?
a) 16 against a 7 up.
b) 16 against a 10 up.
c) 12 against a 2 up.
d) 12 against a 3 up.

4

6) When you have an Ace/7 against a 6 up, odds are you will win 16 times out of 25 if you stand and 15 out of 25 whether you hit or double down. Therefore, you should:
   a) stand.
   b) hit.
   c) double down.

7) You are playing alone against the dealer. Your first hand off the top of a six deck shoe is 2/5/5/4 against the dealer's 10 showing. Your correct play is to:
   a) stand.
   b) hit

8) A pair of 8's against the dealer's 10 up should be split because:
   a) it increases your advantage over the dealer.
   b) it decreases your overall disadvantage.
   c) it turns a losing situation into a "break even" proposition.

9) Which of these hands would you rather have?
   a) 20 against a deuce up.
   b) 20 against a 5 up.
   c) 20 against an 8 up.

10) You're playing two hands alone against the dealer in a single deck game. Off the top of a fresh deal your first hand is Ace/9, and your second is 5/3. The dealer has an Ace showing. What's the first thing you should do?
   a) refuse insurance.
   b) insure both hands
   c) insure the Ace/9, but not the 5/3.

5

11) You've been dealt a blackjack and the dealer has an Ace up. What should you do?

a) *just wait and see what happens.*
b) *double down.*
c) *call for "even money".*

12) You are playing three-handed in a typical six deck game. On the first hand of a new shoe the dealer has a 3 up. The first player splits a pair of 6's and finally stands with 14 and 15 after taking two hits to each 6. The next man doubles down with 9 but catches a baby. You finally stand with 5/2/3/6. The dealer then proceeds to make a five card 21! What's your next move?

a) *leave immediately and look for a better table.*
b) *stay put and increase your bet on the next hand.*
c) *sit out of the next couple of hands and see how the dealer's running.*

ANSWERS

1) **C:** a "stiff" is a hand that can be busted with the next hit. That's 12, 13, 14, 15 or 16.
(score 1 point)

2) **C:** the last seat to act before the dealer is referred to as "3rd base". It's right next to the discard tray.
(score 1 point)

3) **A:** a soft hand is one that contains an Ace counted as 11. If the next hit brings your total over 21, then the value of the Ace can be reverted to "1", hence the term *"soft"*.
(score 1 point)

4) **C:** A 5 will convert every dealer's stiff into a made hand. Computer studies show that a surplus or shortage of 5's shifts the game's percentages more than any other card. (See page 109).
(score 2 points)

5) **A:** 16 vs. a 7 up is the hand most likely to be converted from a loser into a winner by hitting it. The other three hands are all significantly closer calls. (See page 73).
(score 3 points)

6) **C:** Double down! Winning 15 hands out of 25 for $20 each makes more money than winning 16 out of 25 for $10 each. There are numerous situations in blackjack where the most likely way to win is not the most profitable overall play.
(score 2 points)

7) **A:** Stand! With a 10 up, the dealer's average finishing hand will be just over 19 *(barring blackjacks and bustouts)*. You need a 4 or 5 so badly in this spot that their modest depletion now forces you to stand! (See pages 95, 96).
(score 3 points)

8) **B:** Over time, 16 against a 10 actually loses more than twice as much money as 8 against a 10. So your thriftiest decision is to create two 8's and save some money as time goes by. (See page 75).
(score 2 points)

9) **C:** When you have 20 vs. an 8 up, as an 8 to 1 favorite you have the strongest hand you can be dealt where the outcome is not yet known. With the dealer's tendency to have 18, plus the times that she will be pat with 19 by turning over an Ace in the hole, there are very few

7

draws she will ever make to beat your 20. With the other two hands you are between a 4 and 5 to 1 favorite on each. (See page 90).
(score 2 points)

10) **B:** Although insurance is usually a bad bet, with the cards that have come out you should now insure both hands. That's strictly because more than one-third of the remaining cards are now 10's *(16 out of 47)*. It doesn't matter how good or bad your hand is. With more than two decks in use however, an advantageous insurance situation is virtually never available unless you're a card counter. (See page 83).
(score 2 points)

11) **A:** Remember the last sentence from answer #6? This is the classic example of that principle. If you call for insurance and accept "even money", you will gain exactly one bet every time. But if you just take your chances, although you will win some and tie others, you will average winning more than one bet per hand. (See page 75).
(score 3 points).

12) **B:** In blackjack high cards help the player and low cards favor the dealer. At the start of any fresh pack, there are an equal number of each. With the barrage of small cards that have come out here, the remaining pack favors the player. Stay and increase your bet for the next couple of hands. (See Chapter 7).
(score 3 points).

IF YOU SCORED:

0 to 5 points: you're probably better off playing the lotto!

6 - 8 points: a little bit of knowledge is a dangerous thing; for you!

9 - 13 points: you have an average understanding of the game of blackjack; a typical overall contributor to casino profits.

14 - 19 points: you're a fairly solid player and make your wins here and there.

20 - 25 points: you're far above the norm and probably give the house a serious run for its money on a consistent basis.

IN THE BEGINNING....

It was the spring of 1975. My wife and I had been married for eleven years, and we'd never been able to afford a real vacation. Now in our early thirties, we had finally socked enough away to leave the kids with Grandma and Grandpa to go on our own private little "honeymoon". And what better place to get away from the hustle and bustle of everyday life than the adult "Disneyland" of Las Vegas?

Once aboard the airplane, I pulled out a paperback book my neighbor had given me to "browse" through before playing in the casinos. I was relatively new to gambling and surely, could use a few pointers. The book was entitled *"Beat the Dealer", by Edward O. Thorp;* a text on how to gain the edge at blackjack by keeping track of the cards. I opened it to Chapter One, and things would never be the same for me again.

Blackjack made so much sense to me I wished I had invented it! Since then I've analyzed and practiced the game with an intense passion, taught private lessons and done public seminars. I play blackjack regularly, in the midwest and on my visits to Las Vegas and Atlantic City.

Most blackjack books make winning sound easy. It's not! I have written this text in a straightforward factual style that should tell you what to expect when you dedicate your time and effort to playing casino "21". Many game situations are addressed that don't appear in most other books. The strategies are accurate. The illustrations are vivid. Whether you're just fine-tuning your basic strategy, learning how to react to key cards as they fall, or mastering a complex card counting system, I trust you'll find *The Blackjack Bluebook* a most instructive and helpful guide.

10

SECTION A

the Unique Nature of Blackjack

1
Why Blackjack?

Of all the casino games on the floor, why gamble your money on blackjack? After all, what would make *"21"* different from any other casino-banked game?

First off, you need to remember that casino games are the product of a business that was created to make money for its owners. In theory, these games were intended to be mathematically impenetrable over the long haul. You're not really supposed to have a shot at beating the house once everything evens out. The casino can best achieve this "unbeatable" status through games of chance that involve the element of "replacement", such as craps or roulette.

"Replacement" means that when a roulette wheel is spun, if number *23* comes up, that number is *not* wiped off the wheel for the next spin. Likewise, when the number *6* is rolled with a pair of dice, all the faces that add up to *6* also remain available for the next roll. It would be like dealing the Ace of spades, then shuffling it back into the deck before dealing the next card. Consequently, numbers *23* and *6* are just as likely to recur on the next try as they were before. This replacement feature makes craps and roulette games of *"independent events"*. Since there's no process of elimination, no number is ever "due". So the odds never change for the next spin of the wheel or roll of the dice.

With this knowledge in their pockets, in order to gain the upper hand, the inventors of the game only have to pay you odds that are a bit shorter than those *constant* odds against that number coming up. Here's a basic example.

Since there are 38 numbers on an American roulette wheel, the odds against number *23* being spun *(or any other number)* are 37 to 1. And the payoff odds for picking a single number are 35 to 1. Betting a single number, after 38 *averaged* spins of the wheel you'll have 37 losers and one winner. By offering only 35 to 1 payoff odds, the house knows it will have a 2 slot edge on you at *all* times. This 2 slot difference between your payoff odds and the odds against hitting your number becomes the reason why the house wins and the players lose in the long run. And it's all because of something called.........

The BASIC PRINCIPLE of PROFITABLE GAMBLING

You see, for every dollar lost in gambling there is a dollar won. Right now as you're reading this, somewhere in the world two people are betting on something. Chances are, somebody has the edge while the other person is at a disadvantage. The *Basic Principle of Profitable Gambling* is what determines who's who. In short, that principle states that: *In order to gain the edge on a bet, your payoff odds must be higher than your odds against winning it.*

13

Suppose I were to set a deck of cards on the table, then challenge you to cut the deck and name the suit of the card you were going to cut. If I offered you even money, let's say my $1 against your $1 would you take that bet? Of course you wouldn't! You'd refuse it because it's easy to see that you'll lose a buck more often than you'll win one.

But what if I offered $50 to your $1? Now you should certainly bet me! That's because even though you'll usually lose, you'll more than make up for it when you finally do win. How do you know? With four suits in a deck of cards, you have three ways to lose and one way to win. That makes odds of 3 to 1 against winning your bet. Over time, you will in fact lose your bet three times for each winner you make.

Now, what would happen if you were paid $3 each time you picked the right suit, and lost $1 every time you were wrong? You'd break even wouldn't you? So when your payoff odds are *equal* to the odds against winning your bet, you have an *even gamble*. If your payoff odds are higher, you have the edge. And if they are lower, you are at a disadvantage and destined to lose over time. *That's the basic principle of profitable gambling.*

Every wagering proposition in casino games of independent events is based on this "short payoff" principle. When you're getting even money to bet "red" at roulette, you have 18 reds to win with, and 18 blacks plus 2 greens that beat you. That's 20 to 18 against you! If you bet black, you have the same deal. They have you coming and going! And when you bet on number 7 at craps, a win will return five times your money, but the number 7 will only come up one time out of six on average! Even on the ever-popular pass line at craps, the odds to win even money are *always* 251 to 244 against the player. In every case you're

14

on the short end the the Basic Principle of Profitable Gambling. And as difficult as it may be to accept, there is no way to overcome this by following trends or streaks, since the wheel and the dice have no memory whatsoever. Yes, streaks do occur, but there is no way to predict the arrival of one. And once you've established that you're in a streak, it's been demonstrated over and over again that it's just as likely to reverse itself right now as it is to continue. Also, no matter what you may be inclined to believe, there is no *"accountant in the sky"* forcing short term results to *"even out"* when they become unbalanced. That's because:

LOP-SIDED RESULTS ARE NOT CORRECTED; THEY MERELY FADE INTO THE PAST.

Remember that last statement. It's one of the most important things you'll ever learn about gambling. The house is so certain of it that many casinos are cordial enough to post an electronic tote board displaying the last 15 or 20 roulette numbers to come up. At the mini-baccarat table, there are pre-printed forms and pencils with which you can track dealer and player streaks. Is the house giving you information to beat them with? Hardly! In effect, they are telling you, "Go ahead and chart all the past results you like". They know it doesn't make any difference, *and so should you!*

Also in roulette, craps and even baccarat, once you put your money down there is absolutely no way to influence the outcome of your bet. You have nothing to do now but wait for the result. At this point, they are games of *pure* chance. With these factors working for them, the house has a truly *bulletproof* gambling arrangement. They simply have you betting the short end of the stick! Short term fluctuations will literally force the player to win some

15

of the time. Eventually though, the law of large numbers must be adhered to and the casino will come out on top.

The UNIQUE NATURE of BLACKJACK

Now, blackjack is different from this in two very important ways. First, it is one of the few casino games in which the player uses his judgment to make decisions *after* his bet has been placed. These decisions will either increase or decrease his chance of winning the bet. For example, if you always stand when you have *2-4-Ace* against a dealer's *4* up, you'll only win 46% of those hands, but if you hit you'll win 53% of them. Hence, for you blackjack may be the best game in the house, or the worst one depending upon how well or how poorly you make your decisions.

It's true that some of the newer games like Caribbean stud or Let it Ride also offer the player the opportunity to make strategic playing decisions. But these games are modern day inventions, developed according to a completely known set of mathematical probabilities. The house has you right where they want you when you're playing "perfect" Caribbean stud or Let it Ride; at a $2^1/2$ to 3 percent disadvantage!

On the other hand, the game of blackjack is more than a century old. When its rules were first structured, putting the house at an advantage was much more complicated than just paying 35 to 1 on a 37 to 1 shot. The game's inventors had no computers to determine what the exact percentages would be in many of the more extreme nuances that can arise in a blackjack hand. Instead, they had to work from a more fundamental set of mathematical probabilities realizing that the player too, would be limited by his own reasoning powers. That being the case, the

16

available design tools of their day were sufficient to provide the house with a comfortable edge over any human of that era. And so it went for several decades. Then came the age of computers.

Today's computer-derived playing strategies for blackjack extend well beyond the players' own perceptive logic. In a casino gambling arena, where house advantages on table games average about 3%, a well-informed blackjack player gives up just a $1/2$% edge to the house in a typical multi-deck game by doing nothing more than memorizing a basic strategy chart. A $1/2$% disadvantage means playing 200 hands and finishing one bet behind if the odds run perfectly true to form. I don't think it was ever intended to be that close of a contest.

The second big difference about blackjack is, unlike craps and roulette, it is a game of "dependent" events. That means once you've been dealt a *4* and a *3,* then hit it with a *deuce, deuce, 5* and a *6* for example, those cards go into the discard rack and *cannot* be dealt again for the remainder of the shoe. As the cards grow more and more depleted, sometimes certain hands become easier to make and certain other hands grow more scarce. In fact, there are times when your chances of being dealt a blackjack are 1 in 17, and other times when they are 1 in 25. This kind of thing *never* happens in craps, roulette or Caribbean stud. It's like knowing that the number *10* in craps now has one chance in *nine* of coming up rather than the normal one chance in *twelve*. These things do happen repeatedly in blackjack, and can make your odds against winning the next hand shorter than your payoff odds. And that can put you on the right side of the Basic Principle of Profitable Gambling. Of all the house-banked casino games, these are the reasons why you would choose blackjack on which to gamble your money.

17

Chapter 1
KEY POINTS

1) For every dollar lost in gambling, somebody wins a dollar. And in every gambling proposition, somebody has the upper hand.

2) The casino strives to market products with the edge on their side. This is most easily accomplished with games of "independent" events like craps or roulette.

3) With most casino games you make very few or no decisions after you've placed your bet. In blackjack, your decisions greatly affect the outcome of your wager.

4) In most other casino games, the odds never vary from one bet to the next. In blackjack the odds keep shifting with the removal of every card.

5) Because of numbers 3 and 4, the odds against winning your next hand are sometimes lower than your payoff odds. This can put you on the right side of the basic principle of profitable gambling.

6) Blackjack and live poker are currently the only table games in the casino in which the player can gain the upper hand.

2
The House Edge

Before you can intelligently attempt to beat the casino at blackjack, you have to realize where the house edge comes from in the first place. In this game, you're not just betting with 18 ways to win and 20 ways to lose the way you are with *"red"* in roulette. And you're not taking 5 for 1 odds on a 1 out of 6 shot like you are when betting on number *7* in craps. Even on the pass line at craps although it's a much closer bet, all shooters good and bad alike still have the worst of it; every single time they roll the dice!

Blackjack is not that simple, and it's not that absolute. There are thousands upon thousands of variables involved. But still and all at first blush, things seem pretty even. You're trying to make *21* and the dealer's trying to make *21*. You draw cards and the dealer draws cards. If you both get *18*, it's a "push". What could be fairer?

Well, things would be a lot fairer if you could get a "push" on *22*; or on *26*! But that's not how it is. You see,

19

the house draws its edge from the fact that the player must act first! This is the casino's *sole* advantage in blackjack. Because of this, if the player breaks, the house wins right now; even if the dealer would have busted had he been forced to play out his own hand! If the player decided to play his hands the same way the dealer plays his, simultaneous busts would occur 8% of the time. There's the house's initial edge.

So, what can you do about that? If you decide to counteract it by never busting yourself, the dealer will make more "*17* or better" hands than you will; sort of a catch "22". It's impossible to compensate for having to act first, when the first one to break automatically loses. All else being equal, acting first is a *huge* disadvantage; an 8% disadvantage! That would be 50% higher than the house edge at American roulette, which is an awful gamble!

But alas, all else is *not* equal. Apparently realizing that this would be too big an edge for the house, the designers of the game decided to give some "perks" to the player that the dealer doesn't get.

The following table outlines the differences in the rules between the player and the dealer, then defines where the advantage lies for each difference.

WHO HAS THE ADVANTAGE?

PLAYER	DEALER	ADVANTAGE
acts first	acts last	dealer
3 to 2 on blackjack	even money	player
hit/stand at will	must hit 16/stand 17	player
may double down	no doubling	player
may split pairs	no splitting	player

20

As you can see, blackjack is a game with considerably uneven rules. Also, notice that except for having to act first, every difference in the rules favors the player. But because the dealer has no options whatsoever, he is simply an agent of the unwavering rules that he must follow. Therefore, every dealer is just as *tough* as any other. Consequently, the edge that the house may have against any given player is ultimately determined by how efficiently that player uses his options.

So, starting with an initial house edge of about 8%, the player begins to peck away at his disadvantage by using his options the best way he knows how. The next table will tell you in round numbers, how much of an edge each player option is worth if you use it to maximum efficiency.

MAXIMIZING the PLAYER'S OPTIONS

3 to 2 bonus for blackjack	regain 2¹/4%
Proper hitting/standing	regain 3¹/4%
Proper doubling down	regain 1¹/2%
Proper pair splitting	regain ¹/2%

The first thing you'll notice from the table is that the 3 to 2 payoff for the player's blackjacks will eat into that basic 8% dealer's edge by about 2¹/4%. This one's an automatic; you can't mess it up. But the remaining three options are up to you to use wisely, or they will just turn out to be more rope for you to hang yourself with. As the table illustrates, if you can just learn to hit, stand, double down and split properly, you'll reduce the casino's mathematical advantage down to roughly ¹/2% in a multi-

21

deck shoe game with typical blackjack rules. With one or two decks, the player's disadvantage would be a few tenths percent smaller, and with tighter rules, it would be larger. This house edge is ten times smaller than at roulette and five times smaller than Caribbean stud. In fact, it's small enough that if you did nothing more than play all your hands correctly, you should have 6 winning three hour sessions for every 7 losers you book. And that's without keeping track of any of the cards. You can't cut that close of a deal in any other casino-banked table game, except for when triple *(or more)* odds are taken on the pass line or the come at craps.

The other day I was at the blackjack table with a dealer who stated flatly that she never gambles. I asked her if she carried collision insurance on her automobile. *"Sure!"*, she replied. *"Well there you go!"*, I said. *"You're betting that you're going to smash up your car and if you don't, you lose! Furthermore, you're not getting good enough odds on your premium to make it a profitable bet!"*

You see, for insurance companies to remain solvent they have to collect more money in premiums than they pay out in damage claims. That puts the policyholders on the short end of the basic principle of profitable gambling. The sharpies who figure out what kind of odds they're going to lay you are called "actuaries". The insurance companies are the "bookies". But hey, there are some bets you just can't afford not to make! So in that scenario, we all give our insurance companies the house edge and carry the protection we need.

But in blackjack, with enough expertise it is actually possible to turn the mathematical tables on the house by a very small and delicate margin. That comes in the latter part of this book. For now, let's get on with the basics.

22

Chapter 2
KEY POINTS

1) The mathematical innards of blackjack are much more complex than most other casino games.

2) The player and dealer each abide by their own sets of rules and restrictions.

3) The house gains its sole edge in blackjack by forcing the player to act first.

4) Every other rule difference favors the player.

5) Using his strategy options the player can improve or worsen his chances to win, making blackjack a game of skill.

6) If the player makes all his playing decisions efficiently he can nearly eliminate the house edge altogether.

3

Rules of the Game

Blackjack is the most popular table game in the casino. And since you've purchased a book that is described as being for the serious player, I'm going to assume you already have some idea how it is played. So I'm just going to provide a basic outline of the rules and procedures for casino *"21"* on the next few pages.

Casino blackjack is played on a semi-circular table that usually seats seven players, but there's nothing sacred about the number of gamblers at a *"21"* table. Several casinos also provide some slightly smaller tables with only five betting spots in certain pits. The largest blackjack table I've ever seen was at the Four Queens Casino in Las Vegas. That seated twelve players and required two dealers. A more typical blackjack layout is shown in the illustration on the following page. Pay close attention to the fine print on the playing surface. It doesn't always read identically in every casino.

24

Typical
Blackjack Layout

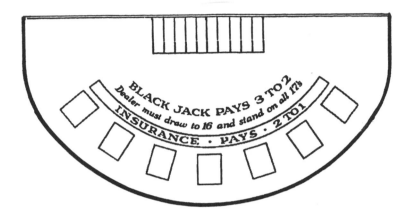

The dealer stands on the flat side of the table and the players sit around the circular portion. These days, the dealer usually deals the game from a *"shoe"* containing anywhere from four to eight decks of cards. But in some places, the game is still dealt with just one or two decks held in the dealer's hand. When *"21"* is played with a shoe, all the players' cards are usually dealt face-up. When it is dealt from the hand, the players cards normally come face-down.

These two separate dealing procedures call for different ways to tell the dealer how you wish to play your cards. In the old days, all the games were dealt face-down from the dealer's hand. This style has come to be known as a "pitch game". The player would pick up his cards and scratch with them towards himself on the table if he wanted another card. If he wished to stand, he would slide his cards face-down underneath his chips.

25

As the years went by, more and more casinos went to the multi-deck shoe games in an effort to protect themselves from card-counters, cheats and to speed up the game. In a face-up shoe game, the players are not allowed to touch the cards. To take a hit you must tap or scrape on the table in front of your hand. If you wish to stand, you must wave the dealer off by passing your hand over your cards.

Notice that in neither case are you required, or even encouraged to speak to the dealer. This is largely because the *"eye in the sky"* wants to be able to oversee the game with a crystal clear understanding of what's going on.

Dealer's Rules

The dealer's rules in blackjack are simple. He has no options and might as well be a robot. If he has less than *17*, he **must** take a card. If he has *17* or more, he **cannot** take any cards. If, in taking more cards the dealer goes over *21*, he automatically loses to any player who is still in the hand.

The only sticky part is when the dealer turns up a hand like the one pictured below.

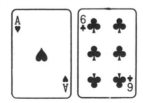

This is called a *"soft 17"* because and *Ace* may be counted as *1* or *11* in blackjack. Many players call this hand *"7 or 17"*. But each casino decides to call it either one or the other when it's in the dealer's hand. If the printing on the table reads, ***"Dealer must stand on all 17's"***, then he must stand when he turns up an *Ace/6*, and his hand is finished at *17*. If the table printing reads, ***"Dealer must hit soft 17"***, then his *Ace/6* is regarded as *7* and he must hit it. The same principle applies if the dealer turns up an Ace/2, hits it and catches a 4. This is still a *soft 17* and falls under the same set of rules.

The funny thing is, if the dealer hits his *Ace/6* and catches an *Ace*, he doesn't have *8*, but *18* and now must stand. As you might guess from the sound of all this, hitting a *soft 17* is to the dealer's advantage. You would prefer to play in a casino where the dealer stands on *all 17's*.

Player's Options

The player has at least four options that the dealer doesn't have. They are listed below.

HIT/STAND: The player may always stand or hit as he sees fit. If he goes over *21* while taking a card, he automatically and immediately loses. It doesn't matter if the dealer goes over *21* afterwards. As soon as the player busts, his chips are raked in, and he's out of the hand.

DOUBLE DOWN: Sometimes the player is dealt two starting cards that are not a complete hand, but have good potential to make a powerful hand with one more card. A classic example of such a hand is shown next.

27

An initial hand of *11* is a powerful start because 30% of all the cards are *10's (10's, Jacks, Queens and Kings)*. Thus, the next card will make *21* almost a third of the time. Even an *8* or a *9* will make *19* or *20* respectively; all good hands.

On his first two cards, if the player thinks he has the advantage over the dealer, he may double his bet, and take one more card. The conditional trade-off for being permitted to increase his bet *after* seeing his cards is; one hit is *all* the player can take! If he catches a *deuce* on his *11*, he's stuck with *13*. Nevertheless, doubling down is a boon to the player in the right spots.

In most casinos, the player can double down with any two starting cards. This would include hands like *Ace/4*, or *5/3*. But a few houses limit your doubling down to certain hands, such as totals of *9, 10* and *11* only. It's better for the player if he can double on any two card holding.

SPLITTING PAIRS: Anytime the player is dealt a pair on his starting hand, he may opt to split them into two separate hands of one card each, and play them out individually if he thinks that's the better way to go. When

28

doing this he will have two bets riding, each one the size of the original wager. A classic example of a good splitting hand would be:

A pair of *8's* is such an excellent hand to split because it breaks up a *16;* the worst hand you can get. You'll learn later on in this book that a pair of *8's* should virtually always be split.

If you should split your pair and receive a third card of the same rank, most casinos allow you to "re-split" by creating a third new hand. Four hands is usually the maximum that can be created by splitting and re-splitting pairs.

INSURANCE: Every time the dealer's up-card is an *Ace,* he is apt to have blackjack. All it takes is a *ten-card* in the hole. If the *10* is there, he's an automatic winner unless you have blackjack yourself, which ties. So whenever the dealer has an *Ace* showing, he will ask the players if they want *"insurance".*

Insurance is a side bet you can make, separate from the wager on your hand that the dealer does in fact have a *10* in the hole for a blackjack. That's right, if the dealer has blackjack you win the side bet, and if he doesn't, you lose. Hence, the term, "insurance". It's a hedge bet.

The price of insurance is half the amount the player has riding on the hand, and it offers *2* to *1* payoff odds if it wins. That price combined with those odds will typically break you even on the hand if you take insurance and the dealer has blackjack. Here's how. Let's say you've bet $10 on your hand and were dealt:

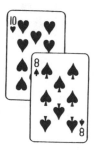

The dealer has an *Ace* showing, so you ante up another $5 by placing it in the insurance ring right in front of your bet. The dealer looks at her hole card, and turns up the *10* of clubs for a blackjack. Now the situation looks like this:

YOUR HAND   DEALER'S HAND

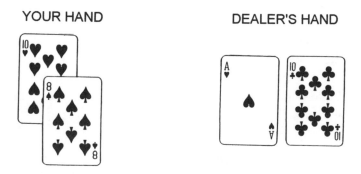

The dealer's *21* beats your *18*, so you lose $10 on your hand. But you've won the $5 insurance bet at *2* to *1* payoff odds, collecting $10 there. All in all, you break even. The same thing would happen if you had *7* or *12* instead of *18*.

There is one other case however, in which you don't break even. It's when you've been dealt a blackjack yourself. Now, if the dealer has the *10* in the hole underneath his *Ace* and you've taken insurance, things look like this:

YOUR HAND   DEALER'S HAND

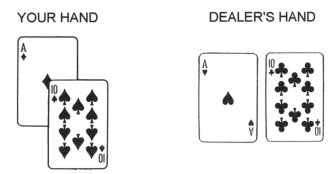

Your hands tie and no money is exchanged there. But you still win the $5 insurance wager receiving *2* to *1* odds thereby netting a $10 profit. But what if the dealer doesn't have blackjack? Let's take a look:

YOUR HAND   DEALER'S HAND

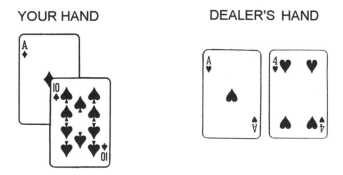

31

Now you beat the dealer and get paid *3* to *2*, or $15 for your blackjack. But you lose the $5 insurance bet, once again netting $10 on the dual transaction! So whenever the you have blackjack and the dealer has an *Ace* up, if you take insurance you will win the amount of your original wager whether the dealer has a *10* in the hole or not. It's no wonder that nine out of ten blackjack players make this play every time. It's a sure thing! However, in Chapter 5, we'll learn why it's the *wrong* play!

SURRENDER: This fairly uncommon option is probably offered in only 15% to 20% of the casinos in the country, but is worth mentioning for its strategic value. On your first two cards, providing the dealer doesn't have blackjack, you may give up half your bet and get out of the hand if you don't like your chances. A classic surrender hand would be the player's *16* against a dealer's *10* up. You would take the surrender option any time you think that losing half your bet is less of a liability than playing the hand out. In Chapter 5, we'll learn that there are indeed a handful of situations that should be surrendered if the option is available.

Many other "specialty" rules are occasionally in force at various casinos, but don't affect the game appreciably. Here, you have been given a "nutshell" summary of how standard blackjack is played in gambling houses throughout the U.S.A., and most casinos abroad. In Chapter 5, *(The Basic Strategy)*, you'll learn how to take maximum advantage of those rules.

Chapter 3
KEY POINTS

1) Two basically different styles of blackjack are played in the casinos; single or double deck "pitch" games dealt from the dealer's hand, and four to eight deck "shoe" games.

2) All else being equal, the fewer the decks used, the better the percentages are for the player, even if he doesn't keep track of the cards.

3) In some casinos the dealer must stand on all 17's, and in others he must hit a "soft" 17. It's moderately better for the player if the dealer stands with this hand.

4) The options the player may use to manage his hand are hitting, standing, doubling down, splitting, taking insurance and in some casinos, surrendering.

SECTION B

What Makes Gambling Tick?

4
Blackjack Myths

Paying attention to important things that happen at the blackjack table can help you win, but a lot of things that many players focus on so intently cannot really help at all. Gambling does funny things to people. So many well-rounded individuals who run their lives in a deliberate and logical fashion become illogical and superstitious when it comes to gambling. It's ironic that superstition is what brings many people to gambling in the first place, when superstition is one of the very things that can keep them from winning. That's because superstition tends to generate myths. And if you're pre-occupied by myths when you gamble, it will prevent you from noticing and reacting to things that actually do make a difference. It will govern your behavior in an unproductive, and sometimes downright self-destructive way.

A myth is defined as something that is generally assumed to be true but is false. Gambling is full of myths, and blackjack is no exception. If you're going to become a serious blackjack player, you're going to have to get over the irrational instincts that plague so many gamblers. Following are five common myths that you must learn to put behind you at the blackjack tables.

Blackjack Myth #1

"I'm due to win one."

Here's a widespread instinctive belief that pertains to just about any gambling game. It generates from a basic, but almost universal misunderstanding of how chance events work. How many times have you seen a blackjack player sit down and begin to play very poised at first? Then after losing the last 4 or 5 hands before the shuffle, he raises his bet from $10 up to $40 or $50 on the first hand of the new shoe. Why? Because he was, "due to win one", of course! After all, this person knows he has to win a bet sooner or later, so that winning hand must be growing more and more likely with each deal, right? *Wrong!*

Remember, that big blackjack accountant in the sky *(mentioned in Chapter One)* only exists in your mind. The gambling gods couldn't care less about evening out the score. And the law of averages couldn't care less either. The cards don't know you've just lost five in a row, and you're not any more likely to win your next hand because of it*. Sure, things will come close to balancing out eventually because the odds are so close to 50-50. That's a given. But *eventually* is the key word here.

Notice that on one hand I'm proclaiming you're never "due" to win, yet I'm conceding on the other hand that

*Technically in blackjack, because the player tends to do better with high cards, and the dealer wins more often with low cards, then if the player has lost several consecutive hands, there is a slightly elevated probability that he has used up an abundance of small cards in doing so. Hence, there could be a surplus of undealt high cards at this point in the deal. But this is an unrelated and negligible factor, applicable only to blackjack. To consider it here would only be misleading.

---

things will eventually even out. Well, how can both be true at the same time? *Now, listen carefully; this is important.*

If you were setting out to flip a coin 100 times, you would be right to expect 50 heads and 50 tails. But suppose that the first 20 tosses happened to produce all heads. At this point, if you brought in an expert Las Vegas oddsmaker to set an *"over/under"* betting line for how many total heads you're most likely to have at the end of your 100 flips, what should his number be? Should it still be 50 heads? 55 heads? 60? How many? The answer is **60.** Why? Because no matter what's happened thus far, *the remaining 80 tosses should produce 40 heads, on average!* And they *will* produce 40 heads more often than any other total!

"But wouldn't that be a total of 60% heads instead of 50%?", you ask. Yes it would be. That's because those 10 extra heads *(in the 1st 20 tosses)* weren't likely to come up, but they did. Still, the most likely thing to happen next is *always* the most normal thing, nonetheless. So there is absolutely no increased tendency for tails to come up next.

But then, how do things balance out in the long run? *Stay with me, we're almost there.* Let's say that because of your unusual start, you decided to extend this experiment to one million total flips, including the 20 tosses you've just completed. Now how many total heads are you most likely to have when you're finished? Remember, all the remaining tosses should produce half heads and half tails. That would

37

add up to a combined total of 500,010 heads; still the same 10 heads above 50%. Then the overall percentage of heads would be only 50.001% That's what is meant by, *"Lopsided results are not corrected; they just fade into the past."* What has happened here is, the ever-accumulating number of *normal* outcomes has diminished the significance of those first 20 unusual results until they've become virtually meaningless. *And that is the only kind of "evening out" process you can ever rightfully expect!*

If you're going to have a chance to be a long term winner at any form of gambling, the first idiosyncrasy you're going to have to shed is the belief that something is due to happen because of what's just occurred. You may have been losing profusely, but believe me, the rest of the universe doesn't owe you a thing! The cold facts are, if the remaining cards in the shoe give you a 49% chance to win the next hand, then that's your chance of winning the next hand no matter how many in a row you may have won or lost up until now. You must learn to believe this or you will repeatedly be working against yourself. When you gamble, every random outcome that's occurred up to now is *irrelevant history.* You're never "due" to win one!

Blackjack Myth #2

"You can Beat the House by Always Quitting when You're Ahead"

I'm really surprised at how many casino gamblers I bump into who truly believe you can consistently beat the house by simply quitting when you're ahead. That would be far too easy! One good reason it won't work is because there will be plenty of times you will lose your very first bet and never get out in front. On those occasions, you *can't* quit when you're ahead. You've never *been* ahead!

Suppose your game plan was to keep betting the pass line in craps, and quit as soon as you got ahead. Well, if you're flat betting, then after making your first five wagers you'll only be ahead about 48% of the time. One-fifth of the time you'll already be at least three bets behind. And you're an underdog on every next bet! If you don't hit a little streak soon, you'll be in trouble.

I've heard some faithful crapshooters react to that dice scenario by saying, "You just have to keep the faith until things turn around and you get a few dollars in front, then quit." Let me remind you that we're talking about a negative expectation game here. From any given point in time, you're always more likely to slide downhill than climb uphill! Yes, if you persist, you *will* put on a rush sooner or later. But if it's later, your streak will only narrow the gap, not eradicate it.

Here's a graph that paints a rough picture of what trying to play "catch-up" often looks like when you start out losing in a disadvantageous game.

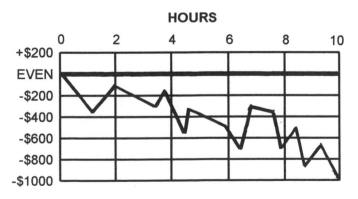

Notice that while you will stage some rallies along the way, eventually you will have fallen so far behind that virtually no winning streak can put you back on top.

But so much for academic analysis. Let's try looking at things from a more practical point of view. It's agreed that during the *majority* of your gaming sessions, you will be ahead at some point in time.

What if your philosophy was to quit anytime your winnings should dwindle to a pre-determined minimum? For example, we'll say you jumped out to a quick $500 lead, then slipped back to being only $200 ahead. Is it a productive strategy to quit right there in order to lock up a guaranteed winner? The answer is; *only if you're never ever going to play again!* But if you're simply going to return on another day and resume gambling, then *there is no difference between that last bet you didn't make because you quit, and the first new bet of your next playing session!* You have the same chance on both bets! And their results will just piggy-back end to end as if it was all one session.

Sound like mumbo-jumbo? Let's try to clarify things with this example. We'll stipulate for a moment that you're rolling *loaded* dice, so that the probability of making a pass is exactly 50% rather than 49.3%. Now your chance of winning some money from any given point in time would be precisely equal to your chance of losing that same amount. When you're $200 ahead, if you keep playing then your chance to eventually go home a $700 winner would be just as good as your likelihood to finish a $300 loser; agreed? Either outcome would have resulted from a $500 change of luck, although in different directions.

Now, if you found yourself in this situation twice, and quit both times in order to "lock up" a couple of winning sessions, your record book would look like this:

Win   +$200
Win   +$200
**   +$400**

That's two wins, no losses and a $400 gain. But instead of quitting, if you played onward both times it would be statistically balanced *(equally likely)* for you to finish a $700 winner one time and a $300 loser the other. Now let's look at the record book:

Win   +$700
Lose   -$300
**   +$400**

Here you would have one win and one loss, but the bottom line is still a $400 net gain. Think *hard* about that. Since you're just as likely to pick up another $500 as you are to drop $500, both events will occur equally often if you always choose to keep playing. That is, you will gain another "X" dollars as often as you will drop that same amount. But it will all net you the same total result as quitting to lock up a winner. What this all boils down to is:

You can't improve your overall chances in a gambling game just by quitting at selective points, then starting up again at a later date.

You see, gambling is not like a basketball game. There, play ends at a specified point, and if you're ahead

100-98 it simply goes into the "win" column without regard for the score. At the start of the next basketball game, the score is always 0-0. But in gambling, when you come back to play next time, you're still ahead 100-98! That's because gambling is really all one long game. There's only one final score and that comes at the end of your life!

Lots of gamblers tell me that when they get back in action the next day, they wipe the slate clean just like a baseball or football game. As far as they're concerned they're starting from scratch again.

Don't kid yourself! Sporting events and gambling are not the same thing at all. There are times you'll see a football team give up more points than it scores during the course of a season, but manage to win more games than it loses and make the playoffs. But if you give up more dollars than you win during the course of a year, no matter how you look at it, *you're stuck!* It doesn't do you any good at all to book 30 small winners if you got *hammered* 25 other times! That's for the sports teams. Indeed, gambling only has one continuous score!

When you quit just to lock up a guaranteed winner, you're only singling out favorable intervals at which to grade your progress. You will succeed however in booking more winning sessions than losers, but they will be smaller wins. *That's because you quit when they became small!* Half of those shrinking wins would have grown larger had you continued to play. And the other half would have shrunk even smaller or become losers, but the bottom line would still be the same, providing you were playing an even game. If you weren't playing an even game, but had a disadvantage, you're still going to lose regardless of your quitting and staying strategies.

By now you may be thinking to yourself, "What's he telling me, don't gamble?" No, I'm not! What I am saying is, "Don't be deluded into believing you can win with irrelevant tactics."

The only way you can become a sustained winner at any form of gambling is to be betting the long end of the stick. That means having a legitimate outright advantage. The more you focus on superstitions or other meaningless game plans, the less aware you will be of things that really do matter. Then you'll just be another frustrated loser, and won't even realize why.

Blackjack Myth #3
"The Order of the Cards is Sacred"

Remember when you were a kid, playing poker on your kitchen table for pennies and nickels? How did you feel when the dealer made a mistake, and you wound up receiving something other than your correct cards? If you're anything like I was as a youngster, you probably felt jinxed.

Well, old beliefs are hard to change. Very often in the casino these days when a new player steps up to the blackjack table in the middle of a shoe, somebody asks him if he would mind waiting until the shuffle. This person's curious request usually stems from that same old fear that the new player is going to corrupt the *"sacred"* order of three or four hundred randomly shuffled cards, and that it's destined to work against the players.

But upon what is this fear based? If blindly changing the order of the cards can work against the player, then why can't it work against the dealer?

Let me ask you this question. If you could hand-pick your cards, face-down from anywhere in the shoe, would you know which ones to take? No, you wouldn't! Then how could you prefer one face-down card over another? And why in the world should the card you would have gotten be *good* for you, but *bad* for the player who actually ends up getting it because of the extra hand that was dealt? It's really no different than when one of the players at the table decides to start playing two hands instead of one, or one hand instead of two. In all these cases, the order of the cards has been changed. And how do you feel when a player at the table suddenly leaves? That's going to change everybody's cards too.

When I play blackjack, even if I knew exactly which cards were left in the shoe, I still wouldn't know their order. So I would never know whether I preferred my own card, or the card of the player next to me. When I double down, it's because based on the *overall* probabilities, taking exactly one more card from *all* those that remain is likely to make a winning hand for me. But I don't know whether the very next card is any more likely to do it for me than the one after it. In fact, I really wouldn't care if the cocktail waitress reached over and pulled it out from the middle of the shoe! I left that superstition at the kitchen table when I was a kid.

Some of the more serious blackjack players have

stated that they only object to the order of the cards being changed when things are going well. And if they are losing, then they in fact *want* to change the cards around so as to break the dealer's "hot streak". This suggests that if you're winning, then the following cards in the shoe are stacked in your favor, and shouldn't be tampered with. But if you've been losing, they're stacked in the dealer's favor.

A fascinating study on just that kind of "streakiness" was reported on in Stanford Wong's highly recommended book, *Professional Blackjack*. In that experiment, 20 million computer hands were run, recording the win/loss results for the player immediately following two consecutive wins, two consecutive losses, and every other possible 2 hand combination of wins, losses and ties. The results; virtually no difference between any of them! The player was no more likely to win his next hand just after having won two in a row, than immediately after losing two in a row. So then, what is there to be preserved in the order of the cards? In that regard, every next hand is a brand new ball game.

More and more in casinos today, signs are showing up on the blackjack tables that read, **"No Mid-shoe Entry"**. That means a new player may enter the game only at the beginning of each new shoe. These signs are more common at the higher stakes tables. Superstitious gamblers say it was done to stop new players from jinxing the incumbents at the table by changing the order of the cards. Now, it *is* possible that casino management may have decided to pacify some of their more superstitious high rollers with this accommodation. But let me tell you, there's at least one much more important reason why those signs are there. And that's to stop card-counters from standing back while

45

counting down a shoe, and then stepping up and making large bets when the deck composition turns favorable for the players. Mind you, deck composition is an entirely different thing than "the order of the cards".

You see, when a card counter does this, it's not because he knows he wants the very next card out of the shoe. He only knows that the remaining cards, in their entirety now contain a lot of *10's* and *Aces*. And that's better for the player than it is for the dealer. At these times, he'd be just as happy to be dealt two cards from the back of the shoe as from the front.

As it all turns out, the casino has the best of both worlds in their **"No Mid-shoe Entry"** signs. They thwart card-counters and appease superstitious blackjack players at the same time.

As for you, don't let the presence of a new player at the table throw you off your game. You have enough to think about without being distracted over things that will only wash out over time. Just play whatever cards you do get the right way, and stay focused on things that you know can make a positive difference.

Blackjack Myth #4
"Bad Players at the Table Hurt You"

Many blackjack buffs are convinced that if another player misplays a hand, it will probably hurt the rest of the players at the table. This belief becomes particularly evident

46

when the player at third base takes a hit to a hand that the other players thought should be held pat. In this spot, if the dealer ends up making a good hand, the 3rd baseman usually receives the blame. Often times, it's loud and indignant blame! I've seen tables practically empty out immediately after the 3rd baseman hit his *14* against a *5* up and the dealer proceeded to make *20*. Have you ever been one of the accusers in this type of situation?

Let's look at this logically. Talk is cheap. It's easy to blame somebody when something goes wrong. But let's try to find out just how much you really believe in what you assert.

What if you were playing blackjack and had stood with *12* against the dealer's *5* up? The player at 3rd base had *14*, and you of course thought he should stand also. But just before he acted on his hand, he turned to you and asked, "Which card is going to be more likely to break the dealer, the *first* one out of the shoe or the *second*?" What would your most intelligent answer be?

Suppose he announced that he was planning to hit his hand. But because of your objection he would agree to stand only if you would make him a little side bet. He would bet that the *second* card out of the shoe would in fact be worse for the dealer than the *first* one. And you of course would be betting on the *first* card. But he insists that you put up $11 to his $10 for the privilege of dictating how he must play his hand. Now, be honest here. Would you make that bet? If you believe wholeheartedly in the bad player myth, you could turn one bad situation into two good ones by giving the dealer his worst card, and winning a $10 side bet to boot. As for me, I like the other fella's chances better, getting 11 to 10 odds on a 50-50 proposition.

47

Why do I say it's a 50-50 deal? *Play along with me a little further in my silly game.* What if in that same hand, you had somehow caught a glimpse of the dealer's hole card and it was a *7 (giving him 12)?* Furthermore, for the sake of illustration, we'll say there were only two cards left in the shoe and you knew that they were a *9* and a *10*; *but you didn't know their order.* Now, what would you want the player at third base to do with his *14?*

The fact is, if the 9 was the first card you would want the player to hit wouldn't you, thereby giving the breaking 10 to the dealer. And if the 10 was first you would want the player to stand, this time saving the bust card for the dealer. But in the long run, each card will be first about an equal number of times. And you'll never know when it will be which way. So it really doesn't matter to you what the third baseman does!

At this point, the next thing you want to realize is that it doesn't matter whether we're talking about the last two cards in the shoe, or *any two adjacent cards.* So, the same principle applies. Now, this next statement is so important that it appears in enlarged bold print:

The real reason why the 3rd baseman should stand is because his chance to win *his own* hand will be better overall by doing so. But in the big picture, that really doesn't favor or handicap *YOUR* hand!

As you can see, when Mr. 3rd base hits in this particular example, no matter which card comes first, he busts. And if he stands, he's got a 50-50 shot at winning. But because you never know which of the two cards is next, *your* hand averages out the same whether he stands or hits! It's true, this whole scenario has been set up artificially, but

48

it typifies the working components of real-life blackjack nuances.

In reality, when Mr. 3rd base has *14* against a *5* up, he will win 34% of the time if he hits, and about 43% of the times that he stands. And if you have already stood with your *12*, you'll win about 43% of the time whether the 3rd baseman takes a card or not.

If a part of you still clings to the belief that a bad player is bad luck for the rest of the table, then how would you handle the following problem entitled:

"The Riddle of the DEALER'S BUST CARD"

Envision yourself playing third base with three or four other players at the table. The dealer has a *4* showing and everybody else has stayed pat with *13's*, *14's* and *15's*. You have a *10/deuce* and aren't quite sure whether you're supposed to stand or hit. But as you're thinking it over, this irrepressible voice inside you keeps whispering; *"Don't take the dealer's bust card".* You dread that the next card coming off may be a picture. The man just to your right has wagered $1000 on his hand and holds *13*. As you look across the table, the other players' eyes seem to be saying, *"Save the table".* Finally, you decide to stand when;

THE DEALER SUDDENLY REACHES INTO THE SHOE AND REVERSES THE ORDER OF THE FIRST 2 CARDS!

Quizzically, you look to the other players. They remain in stone silence, but you can literally read their minds; *"Save the table; don't take the dealer's bust card."*

But which card is the dealer's bust card now? In fact, which was the dealer's bust card before?

49

The truth is, you *never* know which card is the dealer's bust card, and you can *never* deliberately save the table! Don't worry; if another player could really hurt you by making bad plays, there would probably be two casino employees at every blackjack table. The dealer behind the table, and the shill at 3rd base messing up everybody's chances.

So don't be paranoid about playing with bad players. Sometimes they change the cards for the better and sometimes for the worse. Always play your own cards the way you know gives you your best chance of winning, regardless of what seat you're in. And just shrug off any heat you may get from the other players when you're at third base.

Blackjack Myth #5

"Progressive Betting Systems can Overcome the House Edge"

This one is a real Achilles' heel for many casino gamblers, no matter what their game. It seems whenever gambling strategies are discussed, the subject of *money management* betting will eventually come up.

"Money management" is a term that is often incorrectly used to describe some form of "betting progression". But these two terms really don't fit into the same category at all.

Actually, money management in gambling basically means the same thing it does in life; budget your money, don't get carried away, don't self-destruct. No matter how much has been written about money management, it always simply boils down to *never betting over your head.* Betting progressions are something entirely different!

Every day, hoards of gamblers storm the casinos with some form of progressive betting system they feel should *win* more money than it *loses*, even though it will *lose* more bets than it *wins.* Most of these people seem to realize that if you just sit at the gaming table of your choice and make flat *(same size)* bets all the way through, the house edge will eventually grind you down. This is true. Consequently, they have this instinctive reflex to try to bridge that "edge-gap" by varying their bet sizes according to past outcomes as though they predict future outcomes. *Unfortunately, they do not!*

Specifically, a betting progression involves following a prescribed sequence of sizing your bets. There are "win" progressions and "loss" progressions. With a *win* progression, you incrementally raise your next wager after each win in an attempt to capitalize on your winning streaks. But you always revert to a smaller wager, *(usually one unit)* immediately following a loss.

With a *loss* progression, you systematically increase your wager after each losing bet in an effort to recoup your losses when you finally do begin to win. Then you return to a basic size wager and begin the progression all over again.

It's interesting to note that *positive* and *negative* progressions are based upon *opposite* principles. One system is betting that a streak is going to continue, and the

51

other is betting that it is going to end. It should seem apparent that they cannot *both* work. But the grim truth is, *neither* of them can work! Their problem lies in misinterpreting how streaks behave.

Now, listen up! It's critical that you grasp the meaning of this next statement!

Any streak*, no matter how long or how short is basically as likely to end *right now* as it is to continue.

Think about that. Half of all your streaks end *right now!* What this means is, for every two times you've flipped *3* heads in a row, one of those times the *4th* flip will turn up another head, and the other time the it will be a tail.

And what if you bet right after the toss that made the fourth head? Well, half of those times, the next flip will produce the fifth head, and half the time the streak will end by coming up tails. This is what we mean by, *"Half of all your streaks end right now".*

Mathematical probability says this is true and scientific experimentation has backed it up. Therefore, as far as past outcomes are able to indicate, you're never going to be any more or less likely to win your next bet. So then, what good can increasing your next wager in anticipation of an impending victory do? None! Victory is no more imminent than it was before!

---

*"Any streak" as mentioned in bold print refers to even money wagers; most ideally where the odds of a win and a loss are exactly 50-50 such as with a coin flip. But it also applies to bets like a hand of blackjack or the pass line at craps, where the odds are almost but not quite 50-50. Certainly if a dice shooter has just rolled the number 12 three times in a row (each one a 35 to 1 shot) then it would be 35 times more likely that his "box cars" streak would end on the very next roll rather than continue.

Admittedly, this is tricky stuff. Really understanding the uselessness of betting your streaks is a slippery concept to digest. So let's try to clarify things with an example.

Picture this. You walk up to a casino table where the dealer is flipping a coin. It's an honest coin with equal probabilities for heads and tails. You can bet either side and get even money, hence there is no house edge. If you made flat bets from now until eternity, you'd stand to break even. But instead you decide to use a popular *"1-2-3"* positive betting progression.

With this system you start off betting *1* unit, and stick with a *1* unit wager if you lose. But if you win your first bet, you increase to *2* units. If you win two in a row, go to *3* units and stick with *3* units as long as you keep winning. But you'll immediately revert to a *1* unit wager following any loss. This classic approach is supposed to take advantage of your winning streaks by winning the bigger bets and losing the smaller ones.

On the surface, the system would seem to work because if you made three bets and they went like this;

Win, Win, Win,

you would win 6 units. But if they went like this;

Lose, Lose, Lose,

you would only lose 3 units. So far, so good. Now, what would the results be if you won two of your bets and lost one? How about if you won just a single bet and lost two? Well, that all depends. Take a look at the following list.

Win, Win, Win	+6	
Win, Win, Lose	0	
Win, Lose, Win	0	
Lose, Win, Win	+2	
Lose, Lose, Win		-1
Lose, Win, Lose		-2
Win, Lose, Lose		-2
Lose, Lose, Lose		-3

As you can see, the results for any combination of wins and losses depends upon the order that they come in. These are all the potential outcomes for when you make three bets. No possibility has been left out. Notice that they include the same total number of wins as losses *(12 each)*, which they should since flipping a coin is a 50-50 proposition. Now I have to ask you an important question; and think about this before you answer.

WHICH ONE OF THOSE EIGHT POSSIBLE OUTCOMES IS MOST LIKELY TO OCCUR?

The answer? None! They are all equal! If you bet on 3 coin flips, you're just as likely to draw sequence *#2* as *#4, or #7!*

The results that each of the eight sequences would produce are shown to their right. *Now here comes the interesting part.* Add up all the sequences that produce a gain, and you get *+8* units. Add up all the sequences that produce a loss, and what do you get? You get *-8* units.

Now let's stop and think about this. We know that all eight of these sequences are equally likely to occur. Some of them yield a gain while others produce a loss. But if we were to bet on three coin flips *eight different times* and got every sequence once each, where would we be?

54

We would be dead even! And if we were just flat betting all the way through, and drew all eight of these sequences once each, where would we be? Dead even again!

Well the thing of it is, for any three consecutive bets you make over your lifetime *(on a coin flip)*, each of these sequences stands to come up a like number of times! And after they do *you will be even on those wagers combined,* whether you were flat betting, or using a *1-2-3* progression!

Heavy stuff, ugh? And that's not all! *You would also be even no matter what betting progression you used!* Go ahead and try your favorite system out on the win/lose chart right now. It doesn't matter whether it's a win progression, a loss progression or a regression system!

But guess what? There's still more*! It also doesn't matter whether you've made 3 bets, 4 bets, 100 or 1000 bets!* Because for every group of bets no matter how large or small, there are just so many possible win/lose *orders* that they can come in. With *3* bets, there are *8* possible ways for things to come out. With *10* bets there *1024* ways. And with *100* bets, the answer is a thirty-one digit number. But if you laid them all out on paper, and added together the gains from all the profitable sequences, they will always equal the total losses sustained by all the losing sequences! And when you gamble you'll be just as likely to draw any one of them as any other. *You'll simply be getting one small random piece of a very big pie whose pieces add up to zero!* What does all this mean in the end?

No betting system based simply on previous wins and losses can alter the edge of a gambling proposition one way or the other!

But you must understand. Progressive betting systems are not *losing* systems. Indeed they are *"break even"* systems. When betting progressions lose in casino games such as roulette or craps, it's not because they are losing systems. It's because they are "break even" systems used in a losing game! Betting on a coin flip, you will win 50% of your wagers. Betting "red" at roulette, you will win 47.4% of your wagers. Over the fullness of time, *betting progressions will merely yield a result in accordance with the percentages of the game they are being applied to.*

Proponents of progressive betting systems are quick to say that gambling is dominated by streaks, and that is where betting progressions make their money. The truth is, although streaks do occur gambling is actually dominated more by *"switches"* rather than streaks. Switches are that mundane *"win one, lose one, win two, lose one, win one, lose two"* type of process. You can see their prevalence from a quick glance at the win/lose chart. Also notice what happens to your bankroll through a choppy sequence when you're using a positive betting progression. Non-streaky stretches methodically drain a positive progressive bettor's bankroll *even if he wins half his bets!*

A gambler once told me, *"The other night I made nine passes in a row at the dice table and won $2000. I never could have made that kind of money just flat betting".*

What he doesn't understand is, *with positive betting progressions, you win dynamically during your streaks, then piddle it all away through the switches after both modes have occurred as often as they should.* Negative progressions work just the opposite, but the net result is the same.

56

STREAKS and ESP

Still some *"clairvoyants"* insist they can sense a winning streak in the making; that they can actually feel the *"rush"* coming on. Well, this book doesn't deal with ESP. But if they really can do this, then they should increase their bets *only* at these mystical times; *not each and every time they've won a couple in a row!* Because it's an indisputable mathematical fact that about 88% of the times that you *do* win two consecutive bets, you won't reach five in a row. In fact, half the time you won't even win the third bet, and you'll lose your larger wagers in the effort!

Since this is true, any paranormal ability to sense the actual oncoming of a streak would serve an entirely different function than progressing your bets with every single consecutive win *(or loss)*. Progressive betting would be the *"wannabee"* impostor, and ESP would be the real thing.

If all this still sounds a little bit like mumbo jumbo, then imagine betting on that coin flip for one million continuous tosses using your favorite betting progression. When it's over, you will have won virtually 50% of all your bets. Along the way, you will have made tens of thousands of each different sized wager as dictated by your system. But when all is said and done, *you will merely have won 50% of every individual category of bet size!* And that puts you right back to even, doesn't it? Think about it.

Even if there *was* any value to progressive betting, it is particularly ill-suited for a game like blackjack because of all the outside factors that can get in the way. What outside factors? To wrap up the subject of betting progressions, how would you answer the following riddle.

57

PROGRESSIVE BLACKJACK RIDDLE

Suppose you and a friend were both using the same *1-2-3* win progression and sat down at the same blackjack table. There was already a player at first base, then came your friend, an empty seat and finally you.

You and your friend both started off with a one unit wager and both of you won. Next, you each bet two units in accordance with the system, but your friend won and you lost. Now, how many units should each of you bet on the third hand?

Before you answer, ask yourself what would make your friend more likely to win the next hand than you, *against the same dealer's hand.* If you believe that your friend is likely to get better cards than you, then what if just before the cards were dealt, you traded places with each other? Now how many units should each of you bet?

But wait! Does the predisposition to be dealt good cards rest with the player or with the seat? If it's the player, then in order for his luck not to have been severed by this switch, the cards would have to rearrange themselves in the shoe as he changed seats. But if it's the lucky player's position at the table that is destined to win, then what if just before the third hand was dealt, a new player were to sit down between you and your friend just as the player at first base got up and left because he went broke? Now, your friend will receive the ill-fated first baseman's cards and the new player is coming into a seat that has a mini-streak going. How many units should each of them bet?

My answer would be, *"It doesn't matter, without knowing the order of the cards they all have the same chance to win the next hand!"*

58

Chapter 4
KEY POINTS

1) Gambling tends to attract individuals who believe it possesses mystical qualities and secret keys to easy success. It doesn't!

2) The average gambler feels that a string of unusual events is predisposed to swing back in the opposite direction on the other side of normal. It's not!

3) Most gamblers think you can improve your overall cumulative results by quitting at choice intervals, then start up again at a later date. You can't!

4) Many typical blackjack players feel that the order of the cards shouldn't be tampered with. It doesn't matter!

5) Most blackjack players can't let go of the notion that it's "unlucky" to play with bad players. It's not!

6) Nearly all casino gamblers are convinced that following some sort of "betting" system will improve their overall results. It won't!

Gambling has no mind of its own. It has no will or plan, and doesn't give a hoot who wins or loses, today or tomorrow.

Everything you ever bet on will merely be mindless numbers in motion with absolutely no regard for what's occurred up until now. During the course of any wager, its elements are cast into the wind and will come to rest wherever they may, within the confines of their own probabilities.

It's up to you to determine in which direction those probabilities lean and if it's possible, bet on the longer side. *That is the essence of profitable gambling!*

SECTION C

Proper Blackjack Strategy

5

the **Basic Strategy**

In the game of casino blackjack you can be dealt 340 different starting hand situations. When you have *13* and the dealer shows a *6*, that's a hand situation. *16* against a *10* up is another.

About a hundred of these hand situations play themselves. By that I mean, nobody with two brain cells to rub together needs to be told how to play them; they're automatic. Some of these no-brainers are when you've been dealt a *deuce* and a *3* against the dealer's *face-card*, or *19* against a *4* up. A genius and a moron would both play these hands the same way.

But the other two hundred and some odd hands are more debatable. How about when you have a pair of *6's* and the dealer shows a *3?* Should you split them, hit or just stand with *12?* Questions like these should not be answered intuitively, because they are really a matter of mathematics. Unlike some card games such as poker, casino blackjack playing strategy is entirely devoid of psychology.

61

Everyday, thousands of gamblers throw away thousands of dollars at the blackjack tables when they "wing" it by trying to infuse their own personalized logic into the play of their hands. And it's so unnecessary, because all the right plays have already been determined.

The "Basic Strategy" is the mathematically most advantageous way to play each hand you can be dealt in the game of "21" *(without regard for cards that have already been played).*

It has been calculated, simulated, refined and re-refined with computers since the late 1950's. Modern basic strategy was developed by first removing the 3 combined cards that make up the player's starting hand and the dealer's up-card from the "computer" deck. Then, every combination of cards that can be drawn for each way to play that hand was computed and evaluated, indicating the most efficient play. Later, millions of computer simulated hands were dealt, verifying the accuracy of those computations and presto; you have the correct basic strategy of play. With it, the casino's edge over you in a typical multi-deck blackjack game would be just about $1/2\%$. With fewer decks, it would be smaller yet. In some single deck games, a perfect basic strategy player has no disadvantage at all. *(See "Rule Variations" on page 87).*

Without the basic strategy, blackjack would just be another casino table game that has the player hopelessly outgunned. But fortunately, "21" is complex enough that most players make plenty of mistakes, and that's where the bulk of the casino's profit comes from. Hence, the actual percentages themselves don't need to be tilted very far in favor of the house. And indeed they're not, *if* you play your hands correctly.

However, for many people who may be only casually interested in blackjack, playing all their hands correctly is a tall order. Memorizing a complex looking chart full of 260 multi-colored squares can be more work than they care to get involved in. Sometimes, these are folks who merely want to be able to "hang in there" when they play "21" on their next vacation. They're just interested in some sound basics; the fine details can come later.

If that sounds like you, there *is* something simpler than memorizing the complete basic strategy. It's called *"Blackjack's Primary Fundamentals"*. It condenses the entire basic strategy down to just a few fundamental rules.

These are not perfect nor totally complete!

But using these fundamentals, you will still be playing *most* of your hands accurately. There are two levels of *primary fundamentals*; "beginner" and "intermediate". You can learn them in stages on your way to memorizing the complete basic strategy, or stop whenever you've had enough. Either way, you'll be learning to approach the game appropriately.

BLACKJACK'S
PRIMARY FUNDAMENTALS
Beginner Level

1) Stop at **12** if the dealer shows a **6** or lower.
2) Stop at **17** if the dealer shows a **7** or higher.
3) Hit w/ **A/6** or lower and stand w/ **A/7** or higher.
4) Double down w/ **10** or **11** if the dealer shows a **9** or lower.
5) Always split a pair of **Aces** or **8's**, but no other pairs.
6) Never take Insurance.

63

If you can just get these six fundamentals tucked beneath your belt, the casino's edge will have been trimmed down to 1% in a multi-deck game with typical rules. Had you followed the same strategy the dealer plays, your disadvantage would have been over 5%. After you've become comfortable with these simple basics, you can then tackle the somewhat more detailed *"intermediate level"* fundamentals.

BLACKJACK'S
PRIMARY FUNDAMENTALS
Intermediate Level

1) Stop at **12** if the dealer shows a **4, 5** or **6**.
2) Stop at **13** if the dealer shows a **2** or **3**.
3) Stop at **17** if the dealer shows a **7** or higher.
4) Hit w/ **A/6** or lower and stand w/ **A/7** or higher.
5) Double down w/ **11** if the dealer shows a **10** or lower.
6) Double down w/ **10** if the dealer shows a **9** or lower.
7) Double down w/ **9** if the dealer shows a **6** or lower.
8) Always split a pair of **Aces** or **8's**.
9) Split a pair of **7's** if the dealer shows a **7** or lower.
10) Never take Insurance.

Notice that *"intermediate"* rule #1 is in conflict with *"beginner"* rule #1. That's because the *intermediate* fundamentals are more explicit, breaking down your strategy into finer detail. You'll also notice there are more hands to double down with and more pairs to split. Using the intermediate fundamentals you'll be at a $^3/4\%$ disadvantage to the house. That's lower than betting the pass line in craps and taking full odds. It's three times lower than playing "perfect" Caribbean stud, and seven times lower than playing roulette. Picking up the last remaining $^1/4\%$ will be a matter of weaving through a cluster of specific additional pairs that should be split, some soft hands that should be doubled, and a few extra soft hits. When you're ready for those, it's time to memorize a complete basic strategy chart, which follows.

Basic strategies have been developed for single deck, 2 deck, 4 deck, 6 deck and 8 deck games with a number of rule variations for each. Although there is not much difference between any two strategies, it's still nice to have the correct basic strategy for the rules and number of decks you're playing with, so as to get the most you can out of it.

About the most severe possible basic strategy cross-match would be to take a single deck chart that does not allow "double after splits" and has the dealer hitting soft 17, then use that in an 8 deck game *with* double after splits where the dealer *stands* on soft 17. That would cost you about .05%. *(If the 8 deck game also allows surrender and it's not on your chart, you lose another .08%.)*

The color-coded chart on the next page contains the complete basic strategy for the most commonly dealt blackjack games in the U.S.A. It applies to four through eight decks when the dealer stands on *soft* 17. You can double down on any *first* two cards, but *not* after splits and you can re-split your pairs out to four new hands *except* for *Aces.*

65

The

HIT	STAND
DOUBLE	SPLIT

BASIC STRATEGY
4 to 8 decks/ stand on soft 17/ no double after split

DEALER'S UP-CARD

HAND	2	3	4	5	6	7	8	9	10	A
8										
9										
10										
11										
12										
13										
14										
15										
16										
17										
A/2										
A/3										
A/4										
A/5										
A/6										
A/7										
A/8										
2,2										
3,3										
4,4										
6,6										
7,7										
8,8										
9,9										
10,10										
A,A										

66

In some casinos, you're allowed to double down on new two card hands that were created by splitting a pair. A classic example of this would be when you split a pair of *7's*, and catch a *4* on your first *7*, then double down with your new *11*. If the house you're in allows "double after split", then there are seven additional pairs that it becomes advantageous for you to split. The following chart defines those hands with a **"spl"** in the box.

Basic Strategy
When *"DOUBLE AFTER SPLIT"* is allowed

DEALER'S UP-CARD

HAND	2	3	4	5	6
2/2	spl	spl			
3/3	spl	spl			
4/4				spl	spl
6/6	spl				

At some blackjack tables, the dealer must hit a *soft 17*. Even though this tends to improve his hand, he will sometimes bust his *soft 17* when he hits it. Hence, you should double down in these two additional situations.

Basic Strategy
When Dealer *HITS SOFT 17*

DEALER'S UP-CARD

HAND	2	3	4	5	6	7	8	9	10	A
11										dbl
A/8					dbl					

Some blackjack games, particularly in Nevada are still dealt with one or two decks. Following are the hands that should be played differently when playing single or double deck blackjack. **"dbl"** stands for "double; **"spl"** means "split".

Basic Strategy
SINGLE or DOUBLE DECK blackjack

	DEALER'S UP-CARD									
HAND	2	3	4	5	6	7	8	9	10	A
9	dbl									
11										dbl
A/3			dbl							
6/6	spl									

About one casino out of five or six offers the surrender option. The more decks that are used, the more valuable the surrender rule is. If the dealer hits a *soft 17*, the surrender rule is more valuable still. That's because the worse the game is for the player, the less of a chance he has with his bad hands.

Surrender becomes an advantage when your chance of winning the hand gets down to less than 25%. Here's why. Imagine yourself playing four consecutive hands of blackjack with $10 riding on each one. If you lose three and win one, you're $20 behind. If you surrender all four hands, you're still $20 behind. When you win one out of four, it doesn't make any difference whether you played the hands out or surrendered them all.

But if you could win one out of three, you'd do

68

better by playing all three hands out. And if you could only win one bet out of five, it would be cheaper to just surrender all five hands. I'll leave the arithmetic up to you.

Depending upon the rules and number of decks in play, there are between *three* and *seven* blackjack hands that give the player less than one chance in four to win. The following hands should be surrendered in the following games.

SURRENDER
single and double deck

DEALER'S UP-CARD

HAND	10	A
15	sr	▨
16	sr	sr

SURRENDER
4 to 8 decks

DEALER'S UP-CARD

HAND	9	10	A
15	▨	sr	▨
16	sr	sr	sr

SURRENDER
Dealer hits soft 17

DEALER'S UP-CARD

HAND	9	10	A
15	▨	sr	sr
16	sr	sr	sr
17	▨	▨	sr
8/8	▨	▨	*

*SURRENDER w/4 to 8 DECKS

69

Notice throughout the strategy charts how there is a fairly distinct line of demarcation between when the dealer has a *6* for an up-card and a *7* up. That's because when the dealer has a small up-card she will have to draw to get to 17, and may bust while trying. But when she has a 7 or higher up, she is apt to be pat.

As a player, the first thing you should notice when the cards are being dealt is the dealer's up-card, even before you look at your own hand. It sets the stage for how you will play your own cards.

After all is said and done, the dealer will bust 28% of the time. But you can appraise her chances more closely with the information she reveals by turning up one of her cards. The following chart lists the dealer's chance to bust depending upon her specific up-card.

DEALER'S BUST-OUT RATE
(when showing a........)

2	3	4	5	6	7	8	9	10	Ace
.35	.38	.40	.43	.42	.26	.24	.24	.23	.17

These percentages apply to those occasions when the dealer does *not* have a blackjack. If she did, you wouldn't even get to play your hand out. You can see the profound drop between the *6* and the *7*. This is why the strategies diverge so greatly there. Also, if the dealer must hit a *soft 17*, her bust-out rate will be about 44% when showing a *6*, and nearly 20% with an *Ace* up.

70

It's worth your trouble to memorize the correct basic strategy of play instead of going along with popular opinion. In a typical multi-deck game, the average experienced player, making his normal number of mistakes at the table gives an edge to the house of about 2%. A perfect basic strategy player in the same game has a disadvantage of just about $1/2$%. A 2% disadvantage is the equivalent of playing 1000 hands of blackjack and finishing 20 bets behind if all goes normal. With $1/2$% disadvantage, you should be just 5 bets behind. It normally takes about twelve hours to play 1000 blackjack hands. It's not uncommon for many people spend twelve hours at the tables during their vacations to casino country.

If those 15 saved bets don't seem that significant to you, think about this. How many times have you heard people say that when you gamble, you need a little luck to win? But how much luck? Let's express it in specific terms. If you were playing a game where you were supposed to be down 20 bets after making 1000 wagers, statistical probability says that you're a 27 to 10 underdog to be lucky enough to overcome your disadvantage and win anyway. That is, there would be 27 losing players for every 10 winners. But if you were only supposed to finish 5 bets behind, then the odds against you drop to 13 to 10. Having to make up those extra 15 bets with luck is a pretty tall order. Give yourself a better chance. *Learn the right way to play your hands!*

There are many hands that seem to be very frequently misplayed, even by experienced players who consider themselves to be astute at the game. Some of the most commonly misplayed hands I've seen over the years appear on the next page. Without having seen the chart on page 66, how would you have played them?

71

COMMONLY MISPLAYED HANDS

HAND	CORRECT PLAY
12 vs. 3 up	HIT
16 vs. 7 up	HIT
11 vs. 10 up	DOUBLE
A/7 vs. 9 up	HIT
A/6 vs. 6 up	DOUBLE
2/3/A/A vs. 4 up	HIT
9,9 vs. 9 up	SPLIT
8,8 vs. 10 up	SPLIT
Blackjack vs. A up	NO Insurance

How many of these hands did you get wrong? The average veteran of the game misses three. I suspect however, that these errors are not always made out of pure ignorance. Most players know right well that they're supposed to split a pair of *8's* against any up-card. But sometimes, either because there is a big bet riding or just because he's been losing, a player breaks form and doesn't do the proper thing for fear of *"blowing"* two bets instead of one.

Also, I know that lots of players understand you're not supposed to take Insurance on your blackjack, and if quizzed about it will answer correctly. But when it comes to crunch time in the casino, they take the safe way out. Many players talk a better game than they play. Don't be one of them; it will only hurt you. The explanations to the above hands are on the next few pages, and are all mathematically based.

12 vs. a 3 up: This is a hand that ironically, is often played right by novices, but wrong by experienced players. The beginner usually hits simply because *12* isn't much of a hand. The journeyman on the other hand, has learned that when the dealer has a weak up-card he shouldn't carelessly risk busting his own hand and often stands. But *12* vs. a *3* up is in the same ball park with *12* against a *deuce*. With a *2* or a *3* up the dealer is not as weak as when she shows a *4*, *5* or *6*, which are the *only* times you do better by standing with *12*.

16 vs. a 7 up: Most players recognize that the odds basically force them to hit with *16* against a *face-card*. But when the dealer only has a *7* up, many people are less intimidated and sometimes stand with *16*. This is all backwards! It is much more important to hit *16* against a *7* than against a *10*. Why? Because with *16* against a *face-card*, if you're fortunate enough to avoid busting by catching something like a *deuce*, you're still a solid underdog in the hand. But if you catch that same *deuce* against a *7* up, you've probably just made yourself a winner!

11 vs. a 10 up: This is most likely the one double down that most players *wimp out* on. Their major fear is that they may be doubling into a dealer's pat *20*. But did you know that the dealer's chance of having a made *20* is *smaller* than your chance of making *20* or *21* with your very next card? If you just hit, you'll win 56 hands out of 100 for one unit each. If you double down, you'll only win 54 times, but it will be for two units apiece! Doubling is the more profitable long run move.

73

Ace/7 vs. a 9 up: If you played an entire lifetime of blackjack, and stood with a pat *18* on every single hand, you'd die a small loser! And that dealer's *9* up there doesn't make your chances any better. But the *Ace* in your hand gives you some flexibility. If you stand, you'll win eight times out of twenty. If you hit all the way to *a soft 19*, a *hard 17* or bust, you'll win nine out of twenty.

Ace/6 vs. a 6: Some players tend to feel that they already have the dealer beaten with *17* here, so they'd better not push their luck and consequently stand. The truth is, if you just sit tight you're even money to win the hand. But if you hit, you become a 9 to 7 favorite. So then, it would seem that the correct play is to hit, right? *Wrong?*

Ask yourself this question. As you prepare to hit this hand, how many cards can you catch that will make you want to take a second hit? Think it over before you answer.

There are none! Your worst possible card would be a *5* giving you *12*. And with *12* against a *6* up, you're going to stand anyway! By taking exactly one more card, you go from even money to a 9 to 7 favorite. And when you double down it's for twice the money, so double down you must! There are several other *soft* hands that fall into this same category.

2/3/Ace/Ace vs. a 4 up: This is just a generic example of one of the many ways you can build a multi-card *soft 17*. In the confusion of taking extra hits and adjusting the value of their *Aces* along the way, many players get "brain-lock" when they see they've reached *17*, and stand. But a *soft 17* should **never** be stood with! Standing in this particular situation, you'd be an 8 to 7 underdog to win the hand. If you hit you become an 8 to 7 favorite! Hit all your *soft 17's* no matter how many cards they contain!

74

9,9 vs. a 9 up: Some hands are really foolers, and this is one of them. Just as with the *soft 18* on the previous page, this *hard 18* will only beat a dealer's *9* up eight times out of twenty. But *9* against a *9* up is just a tad less than an even money shot all by itself. It may look like a *kamikaze* move, but splitting your 9's will save you some chips in the long run.

8,8 vs. a 10 up: *16* against a *10* up is the worst blackjack situation you will ever find yourself in. You'll only win this hand three times out of thirteen. But when your *16* comes in the form of a pair, you have an escape hatch. Over time, *16* against a *10* actually loses more than twice as much money as *8* against a *10*. So the cheapest way out of this trap is to create two *8's* and save some money as time goes by.

Blackjack vs. an Ace up: Conventional wisdom says, *"A bird in the hand is worth two in the bush"*; *"Don't look a gift horse in the mouth"*; *"Never turn down a sure thing"*. Well, clichés are cute, but they sometimes misrepresent the facts. Taking the *"even money"* guarantee on your *blackjack* when the dealer shows an *Ace* is undoubtedly the most widespread sin committed by the blackjack playing masses. How can I best illustrate this?

Let's imagine you have bet $100 on your hand and were dealt a *blackjack*. The dealer has an *Ace* up. You realize that if the dealer has anything but a *10* in the hole you'll win $150. But if she has the *10*, giving her a *blackjack* too, then you'll tie. You're also aware that you can take insurance, and then you'll win $100 no matter what the dealer has. So you decide to settle for the "bird in the hand" and ask for "even money". But the dealer politely informs you that there is no insurance option in this imaginary casino.

Just then, the player next to you leans over and says, *"Psst, hey pardner; I can see you're between a rock and a hard place. So I'll tell you what I'm gonna do. I'll buy your hand from you right now for $10, win or lose. What'ya say?"*

"Who do I look like, Forrest Gump?", you snap back. *"Unless the dealer's got a 10 in the hole, I'm about to win $150 here; and you wanna give me ten bucks? Get real!*

Now the fella comes right back with, *"Yeah, I guess you're right. Okay, I'll give you $145",* as he slides five green chips and four reds over towards you. As quickly as you possibly can, you scoop up the $145 and wish him luck.

Well, was I correct in assuming that you would reject the $10 and accept $145? Now let me ask you, what two processes did your mind go through in order to arrive at those two conclusions? Maybe you don't really know. Maybe you can just sense intuitively that $10 is a rip-off, and $145 is a bargain, *which by the way, is true!*

This whole make-believe scenario was dreamed up just illustrate an important point. That point is:

THERE IS A PRICE AT WHICH IT BECOMES WORTHWHILE TO SELL YOUR HAND!

But at what price? If you shouldn't sell your hand for $10, but you should for $145, at what price did it suddenly become worth selling?

The proper way to evaluate this is to figure your average gain by playing the hand out. When you have *blackjack* and the dealer shows an *Ace*, four times out of thirteen, she will have *blackjack* too, on average. Those four times, you will tie. The other nine times you will win $150 for an average gain of just about $104 each. This is the *fair market value* of your hand; $104. If you can get more than $104 for your hand, you should sell it. If you can't, *you're better off keeping it!*

When you take insurance on your blackjack, financially it's the same as selling your hand back to the house for $100. That's too cheap, and is why they offer it at every opportunity! *By insuring a blackjack, you'll only reduce the amount of money you make on all your blackjacks combined!* If you needed a guaranteed winner that badly, you have overbet your bankroll. And if you think turning down a "sure winner" is always the wrong thing to do, you don't understand the working mechanics of profitable gambling. Don't make the mistake the house is counting on you to make. Don't sell yourself short. *Don't take "even money" on your blackjack!*

Now that we've covered some specific problem hands in blackjack, let's spread out to some generic hand groups that can cause players a lot of uncertainty.

SOFT HANDS

After looking over the Basic Strategy charts, you might need a helpful tip on playing your *soft* hands. Those are hands that contain an *Ace* when the other cards in the hand total 10 or less. The best way to handle soft hands is to *always* count the *Ace* as *11* unless doing so would bring your total over *21*. Then revert the value of the *Ace* back to *1,* and play your cards like the *hard* hand it has become. And remember, *never* stand on a soft *17*. There, you will always be either hitting or doubling down.

But it's the *soft 18* that is probably the trickiest hand of all to play. That's because depending upon the dealer's up-card, you will sometimes stand, sometimes hit and sometimes double down! The color chart shows this more clearly than anything else.

BAD SOFT DOUBLES

I'm going to take a moment here to say a word about soft doubling down. That's when you double against a small up-card with an *Ace* and a small or medium card in your hand. When I first started playing blackjack and saw other players making this move, I thought to myself, *"What the heck is the idea behind that?"*

Well, basically the idea behind any blackjack maneuver is to play the hand in such a way as to provide the maximum return on your investment. First off, in order for any kind of doubling down to be beneficial you must be more likely to win the hand than lose it. Otherwise, why would you be increasing your bet?

78

But just being a favorite on the hand is not enough to make doubling down the right play. Doubling down must also return a greater profit than playing that hand *any other way!* With many soft hands against a weak dealer's up-card, you make money over time regardless of whether you hit or double. But with some of them, just hitting it makes *more* money! That makes it a bad double down! In some cases you even go from an odds-on favorite to an underdog when you double down instead of hit.

Proper soft doubling can gain the basic strategy player about a tenth of a percent in six deck play, and a tad more with fewer decks. But many overly-aggressive players tend to double down with almost any soft hand against any small up-card. In fact, *I think many players give more back to the house in bad soft doubles than they gain in good ones!* Take a look at the two hands below:

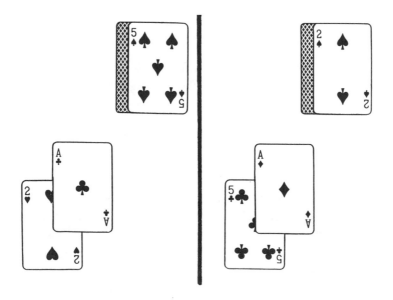

They appear pretty similar, don't they? To the majority of players, these two hands look just about the same for playing purposes. They're not! One hand is moderately good for soft doubling down; the other is a sucker's double!

I find it ironic that a few houses don't allow any soft doubling down. I could follow the casino's rationale if they forbade re-splitting of pairs or doubling after splits. After all, when a player splits a pair of *8's*, then catches the third *8* and is restricted from re-splitting, it costs him money. Also, if he caught a *3* on one of those *8's* and couldn't double down, that restriction would usually cost him money too. But when a player wants to double down with *Ace/5* against a *deuce* and can't, *that costs the casino money!* And people do it all the time! In so many cases, not allowing soft doubling down just saves the bad player from himself!

You should in fact soft double down in 18 situations where you have *Ace/2* through *Ace/7* against a small dealer's up-card. But which ones? Remembering these three simple rules will get you to pull the trigger correctly on 17 of them.

1) **Never** *soft double against a deuce.*
   (where normal basic strategy is concerned).

2) **Always** *soft double against a 5 or 6.*

3) *When the dealer has a 3 or 4 up, play by the* **"rule of 9"**.

What's the *rule of 9?* Simply add together the dealer's up-card and your "kicker" next to your *Ace*. If they total *9* or more, double down! If it's less, just hit. For example, with *Ace/5* against a *3*, add your *5* to the dealer's *3*. This totals only *8*, thus you should not double. But with *Ace/6* against a *3* you should; get it? Oh; the 18th hand not covered by these three rules? You should also double with *Ace/4 vs. 4.*

80

INSURANCE

Taking insurance when you have a blackjack has already been discussed in great detail. Don't take it! But what about at other times? You should *practically* never take it! Why not? Because insurance is basically a bad bet all the way around *(remember the fundamental principle of profitable gambling)*. For every 13 times the dealer has an *Ace* up, she will have a *10* in the hole just about 4 times. If you made a $5 insurance bet on 13 different hands when the dealer had an *Ace* up and she had blackjack 4 times, you'd win 4 insurance bets at $10 each *(2 to 1 payoff odds)*. Then you'd lose $5 the other 9 times for a $5 net loss on the 13 insurance bets combined. This is just a small cross-section of what would happen in the long run for *all* times you took insurance.

"But what about protecting my hand?", you ask. What makes you think you can protect your hand? You've got to get that kind of thinking out of your head! You're always going to win or lose the bet on your hand *just the same* whether you take insurance or not!

No matter how you may view it, when you take insurance you're simply making an additional bet on something else. Any bottom line result that taking insurance combined with the outcome on your hand may produce is purely *incidental!* To place any significance upon that would mislead you into making bad gambling decisions.

Insurance offers 2 to 1 payoff odds on a bet that you normally have less than 1 chance in 3 of winning. That violates the Basic Principle of Profitable Gambling. Knowing this, if you had no bet riding on any hand at all, would you want to make an insurance bet based on its own merit? Of course not! That would be a sucker bet, wouldn't it? Well, just having a hand in front of you doesn't make the insurance bet any better of a value. *The outcome of your hand won't be affected by it one iota, and you'll still lose money on all the insurance bets you make over time.*

INSURE A GOOD HAND??

Some players believe you shouldn't insure a bad hand, but you should insure a good one, like *20* for example. They feel that if the dealer has blackjack, you avoid losing money with a good hand. And without a blackjack, the dealer will have a hard time trying to beat your *20*.

The truth is, all other things being normal, when you have *20* would be the *worst* possible time to take insurance! The reason is, in order to win the insurance bet the dealer has to have a *10* in the hole. But your *20* just took two *10's* out of play *(presuming you don't have Ace/9)!* Now the insurance bet has just gotten worse!

Remember; you shouldn't be combining the results of one bet with another to judge the value of the second bet. When you have *20* against an *Ace* up, you're a 4 to 3 favorite to win money before the dealer even looks at her hole card. You're in a *positive* situation. If you insure a *20*, you're accepting 2 to 1 odds on a bet that is usually about $2^{1}/3$ to 1 against winning. That's a *negative* situation. If combining both those bets together seems like it produces a net advantage, that's because it does; just barely. But the entire source of your advantage came from being dealt a *20!* If you take insurance, you will drag down the overall value of your favorable position to just a bit over "break-even

82

status. *In gambling you should never make a bad bet in an effort to protect a good one!*

INSURANCE for BASIC STRATEGY??

Now, just what did I mean when I said, *"You should practically never take insurance"*? Most blackjack books will tell you to completely ignore the insurance proposition unless you're a card counter. Well, that's *practically* right.

However, even if you don't count cards there are still a few rare opportunities to make an advantageous insurance wager; *but only in single and double deck games!* And it has nothing to do with whether you have a good or bad hand. It only has to do with the odds against winning the insurance bet. Take a look at the illustration below:

It's a single deck game. All the players' cards are dealt face-down. There is just one other player at the table and you have gotten a glimpse at his cards *(which is easy to do)!* Notice that there are no *10's* among either of your hands.

The point here is, it doesn't matter whether it's the first hand off the top of the deck, or you're thirty cards into it and haven't been paying attention to what's been played out. Either way, where you're concerned the dealer could have any one of 47 cards in the hole and 16 of them would be a *10*. That's over one-third winners for you on a bet that pays 2 to 1 odds. *Get some insurance money out there!* You now have a 2.1% edge on the insurance wager instead of the usual 5.9% single deck disadvantage. If there was a third player in the hand and he held no *10's* either, your insurance edge would climb to 6.7%! This is an example of how shifting odds can work to the player's advantage.

Don't be concerned about the cards that may have already gone by just because you don't know what they were. *They are in exactly the same category as the cards still remaining in the deck; unknown!* Even though your information may not be as complete as you would like, *any card you can't eliminate by having seen it is available to be the dealer's hole card!*

How far can you go with this concept? You can even make a good insurance bet when there *are 10's* in the other players' hands if you can see *enough* hands and the *10's* are *scarce* enough!

What about in double deck play? There, it's much harder to find a favorable insurance situation. And beyond two decks it's virtually impossible without counting down the shoe! One help is that some two deck games are dealt face-up. If you're ever playing in a double deck face-up game and you see *nine* cards on the table *(four hands plus the dealer's Ace up)* with *no 10's* among them, take insurance! The same holds true for six hands containing *no more than* one *10*. Your edges here will be 1.1% and 2.2%

84

respectively, instead of the usual 6.8% two deck disadvantage on insurance. And they will be rare occurrences at that. The two deck odds against seeing four hands and no *10's* when the dealer has an *Ace* up are 21 to 1! Dealing six hands against a dealer's *Ace* up with *no more than* one *10* among them is a 15 to 1 shot. Nevertheless, a one or two percent edge is still better than anything else you can find as a basic strategy player. *Take it if you can get it!*

The chart below itemizes the single and double deck opportunities for profitable insurance betting by a basic strategy player. Look them over and remember them if you can. Should one of these situations pop up, *take insurance!*

NO. of DECKS	NO. of HANDS SEEN	MAXIMUM NO. of TENS
1	2	0
1	3	0
1	4	1
1	5	2
2	4	0
2	5	0
2	6	1
2	7	2

Without fulfilling these requirements, you're just going to have to know something about the cards that have passed by on previous rounds in order to find a profitable insurance wager. That comes in the card counting section of this book. Other than that, it's true that a basic strategy player should simply forget the insurance proposition exists.

RULE VARIATIONS

At any casino you walk into, the blackjack games will look just about the same. But when it comes down to the nuts and bolts, each casino has it's own little set of personalized "sub rules". How many decks do they use? Can you double down after splits? How many times can you re-split a pair? Does the dealer stand or hit on *soft 17?* What about "surrender"? In some cases, the rules can detract from the players' percentages enough to make you want to look for a better blackjack game.

Sometimes there are even different rules at different tables within the same casino, usually dependent upon the number of decks that are used in each instance. Multi-deck shoe games tend to have better rules since they are inherently tougher to beat in the first place.

How much difference can the fine points in the rules make? Let's look at the extreme case. About the best game you could ever possibly hope for would be single deck where the dealer stands on a soft *17,* you can double down on any two cards including after splits, you can re-split your pairs out to four new hands, you can re-split a pair of *Aces* if you catch a third *Ace,* and you can surrender. In this *dream blackjack game,* a perfect basic strategy player would actually have a 0.2% advantage over the house. This is the equivalent of being two bets ahead after 1000 hands if the luck of the draw breaks even.

However, a more typical *"real world"* blackjack game would be like that which appears on page 66, *(and is described at the bottom of page 65).* With four decks and

86

those rules, the house advantage would be *0.50%.* Using that as a *reference base,* you can add and subtract the following percentages as the rules and decks vary.

RULE	PLAYER GAIN
1 Deck *(instead of 4)*	+0.50%
2 Decks *(instead of 4)*	+0.15%
6 Decks *(instead of 4)*	-0.07%
8 Decks *(instead of 4)*	-0.10%
Dealer hits soft 17	-0.21%
Double on 9, 10, 11 only	-0.11%
No Re-Split, normal Pairs *(1 dk.)*	-0.02%
No Re-Split normal Pairs *(8 dks.)*	-0.06%
Double After Split	+0.14%
Re-Split Aces *(1 dk.)*	+0.03%
Re-Split Aces *(8 dks.)*	+0.07%
Surrender *(1 dk, stand A/6)*	+0.03%
Surrender *(8 dks, hit A/6)*	+0.10%

The worst available blackjack game within these rules would put the player at just about a 1.0% disadvantage to the house; *a sucker game.* How much would that hurt your chances to win? With *"dream"* blackjack, a perfect basic strategy player's chance to win over the course of 100 accumulated hours of play would be about 55%. With *"sucker"* blackjack it would be 15%. However, neither figure includes player mistakes or dealers' tips; two overhead expenses that come into the picture in *"real world"* blackjack. In scouting a game, if you can find lower than a -0.4% house edge, you've done well. Games higher than 0.6% should probably be avoided by a basic strategist.

87

DOUBLING FOR LESS

It's surprising how creative some gamblers can get at the "21" tables. Unfortunately, blackjack is not a game that lends itself well to spontaneous creativity. In my travels, I've seen some players go far beyond the call of gamesmanship to find ways to hurt themselves while playing blackjack.

One of the most illogical maneuvers I've witnessed is *doubling down for less than twice the original bet.* It usually seems to occur when a player is psychologically torn between hitting and doubling with his hand.

You need to remember that when you double down, you are making a trade-off. In exchange for the right to double your wager in an advantageous situation, you're giving up the right to take additional cards if you don't like your first hit. This will usually decrease your overall number of hands won, but increase your net gain due to the extra action you've put in as an odds-on favorite. But if you don't put the maximum amount up, you're not taking full advantage of your end of the bargain!

As an example, let's take the case where you have made a $15 wager and are dealt an *11* against a *10* up. If you just hit it, you will win 56 times out of 100. And if you double down you will only win 54 times, because if you catch something like an annoying *3*, you're stuck with *14* against the dealer's *10*.

Nevertheless, doubling down is still the right play because winning 54 hands and losing 46 at $30 each makes a $240 profit; where winning 56 and losing 44 at $15 each only nets $180.

88

But what would happen if you *"doubled for less"* by only putting an extra $5 chip up next to your original $15 wager in that same situation? Now you're going to go 54 and 46 for a total gain of $160. *That's the worst of all three worlds!* And it's a common result when you double down for less than the maximum amount. So *never, never* double for less!

TAKING IT ALL IN STRIDE

Now that you have all the concepts of correct basic blackjack play under your belt, you can walk right up to any *"21"* table and know just what to expect whenever you stand, double or split, right? Not really. Surprises abound in this game. I see it all the time; gamblers grimacing painfully or slapping their foreheads.

It seems to happen a lot when they have perhaps a potent looking *11* against something like a wimpy *6* up. Sure, you've got to double down; you have the dealer at a serious disadvantage! But all too often it seems that you catch a baby, and the dealer pulls a three or four card *20*. *"How do they do it?"* , you might exclaim; *"I'm supposed to win that one! What's going on here?"*

What's going on here is you *are* supposed to win that one; *two* times out of *three!* That last part's the key. You doubled down not because you were a lock, but because you had the edge. This is the nature of gambling. You should expect to lose that particular hand once for every two times you win it. It's no big deal!

89

Haven't you ever won a hand when you hit your *15* against a *face-card?* I'll answer that for you. Yes you have; about once for every three times you've lost it if you've played a fair amount of blackjack in your time. When we win those though, it's our nature to dismiss it as a natural by-product of our skillful play. But the truth is, sometimes we get lucky, and sometimes we get unlucky.

Following is a list of common hands along with their associated odds of being won by the player. They should give you a clearer understanding of what you can expect when you play blackjack. Remember that in the short term anything can happen. But over the long haul, your results should come very close to the odds. A 5 to 2 favorite means you should win that hand five times for every two times you lose. A 5 to 2 underdog means just the opposite.

HAND	PLAYER'S ODDS
20 vs. 8 up	8 to 1 favorite
20 vs. 4 up	5 to 1 favorite
19 vs. 3 up	5 to 2 favorite
11 vs. 6 up	2 to 1 favorite
18 vs. 5 up	8 to 5 favorite
10 vs. 2 up	3 to 2 favorite
A/3 vs. 5 up	9 to 7 favorite
19 vs. 10 up*	8 to 7 favorite
A/5 vs. 3 up	even money
17 vs. 7 up	5 to 4 underdog
17 vs. 2 up	4 to 3 underdog
18 vs. 10 up*	7 to 5 underdog
12 vs. 5 up	7 to 5 underdog
15 vs. 2 up	9 to 5 underdog
17 vs. 9 up	5 to 2 underdog
15 vs. 10 up*	3 to 1 underdog
16 vs. 10 up*	10 to 3 underdog

*After the dealer checks his hole card and does **not** have blackjack

Notice that when you have *20* against an *8* up, you should win the hand eight times out of nine *(counting ties as a half win and a half loss)*. When you lose *that* one, you might have a little something to complain about. And with *16* against a *10*, even if the dealer doesn't have blackjack you should still only win three times for every ten that you lose.

These two hands span the entire spectrum of the game of "21", showing you when you have the absolute best and worst of any situation where the outcome is still in question.

Sometime when you're playing blackjack, if you lose on a hand you thought was a real bad beat, come back home and look it up in the book. You might find that you weren't as big a favorite as you thought.

91

Chapter 5
KEY POINTS

1) For the typical player, the Basic Strategy is the most efficient way to play all of his hands. Using it will usually cut the house's percentage edge down to 1/2%.

2) Blackjack's "Primary Fundamentals" are easier to learn at the expense of an additional 1/4 to 1/2% house edge.

3) There are specific basic strategies for different rules and numbers of decks. Not having the appropriate information can cost the player roughly .05%.

4) Taking "even money" on a blackjack when the dealer has an Ace showing is the single most widespread strategic error made in the blackjack playing universe.

5) As a group, the most widely misplayed hands are "soft" double downs".

6) Many experienced players still wrongly believe it's good to insure their *"20"* when in fact, that's usually the worst possible time to take insurance!

7) Although rare, there *are* a few occasions when it is advantageous for the basic strategy player to take insurance.

8) Rule variations and numbers of decks in play can have more than a 1% affect on the overall percentages, but most games fall within a 1/2% window.

9) Doubling down for less than the full amount is virtually always a horrible play!

6

Borderline Blackjack Hands

This is the point at which blackjack starts to become a legitimate game of skill beyond the scope of just memorizing a chart or two. In order to play the *borderline* hands effectively you're going to have to become a bit of a *"card player"* in your own right. Here is where you begin to understand why you hit, stand or double when you do. And through that understanding you'll learn to *"tweak"* your play with certain hands in the right spots. That will condition you to think along the same lines as a blackjack pro.

What are "borderline hands" all about? Well, you've already had a thorough look at the basic strategy. But just looking at a basic strategy chart, it's easy to get the impression that all the correct plays are equally correct. This is not really the case.

For example, the chart doesn't clarify that when you have *12* against a *7* up, you're a 3 to 1 underdog if you stand, but only a 1½ to 1 dog if you hit. It just gives you

93

the information you need to know; *"Hit 12 against a 7 up"*. That's fine, because it's not even close. There is never a time you should even consider *standing* with *12* against a *7!*

But what about when you have *16* against a *10* up? Now, with *this* hand you should win 47 times out 200 if you hit, and 46 times if you stand *(counting ties as a half win and a half loss)*. ***That's a mighty close decision!*** But again, the basic strategy simply says to hit. *There is a tiny problem with this.*

The correct play for this hand was derived by removing either two *10's* and a *6*, or a *7, 9* and *10* from the pack, and then playing the hand out with the *remaining* cards. Working with that, it was found that the player will win about one extra hand out of 200 by hitting rather than standing. Hence, even though it's very close, with a *starting* hand of *16* against a *10* up you should indeed hit.

Notice here, that I said *"starting"* hand. Observe that every one of the cards that were removed from play to make up this hand situation would have busted a *16* if they were still available. However, they are *not* available.

But what about all those times you're dealt *12* against a *10* up, hit and catch a *4* to make *16?* Or maybe you start out with *6/3*, then hook a *5* followed by a *deuce*. How about *4/4/4/4* against that *picture card* showing? If the situation was so close before, should you still hit now? In the majority of cases, the answer is *NO!* But the basic strategy does not take these holdings into account! This is what borderline hands are about. *The following strategies for borderline blackjack hands apply to one through six decks, but are not recommended for eight decks.*

94

COMPOSITION-SENSITIVE HANDS

There are basically two different types of borderline hands in blackjack. The simplest forms are called "composition-sensitive" hands. That means, it matters which specific cards compose your hand.

16 against a 10: Roughly half of all the times you have this hand, your *16* will be the "built up" variety. And counting all its forms, you'll find yourself in the annoying situation of having *16* against a *10* up about one hand out of every thirty over the rest of your blackjack days. That's more often than any other hand!

It was mentioned earlier in Chapter *5* that if you hit *16* against a *10* and are lucky enough to stay alive by catching something like a *2*, you're still probably going to lose the hand. And you will, seven times out of twelve! In this spot, you almost need to catch a *4* or a *5* to be in good shape because of the dealer's tendency to have *20*. But if your *16* contains any *4's* or *5's* in it, you've taken one or two of your key cards out of play. Plus, that means you probably don't have a *10* in your hand which makes one more face-card available to bust you. This fairly subtle change swings the probability pendulum the other way.

The bottom line to all this is, ***against a 10 up, if your multi-card 16 contains any 4's OR 5's, stand!*** Yes, even with six decks. A *classic* stand situation would be a *16* made up of *7/5/4*. But if you have built something like an *A/6/8/A*, you should still hit because you haven't drawn any cards out of play that would have done much for your hand. Here are two vivid illustrations to help clear things up:

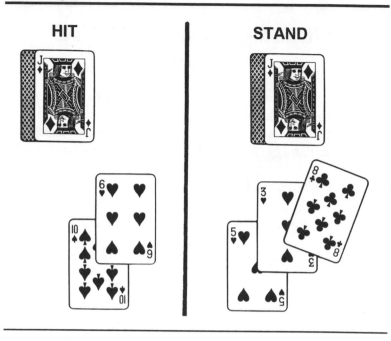

12 against a 4: This is another very marginal hand. Nearly all blackjack books recommend standing with *12* against a dealer's *4* up. That's because the overall odds are, you will win 120 times out of 300 if you stand and 119 times if you hit *(again, adjusting for ties)*. *But the problem is, there are four different ways you can be dealt a 12!* They are *10/2, 9/3, 8/4* and *7/5*.

Notice the striking difference between holding a *10/2* and a *7/5*. With the *10/2* if you hit, you can catch the *7* or the *5* that would have been *unavailable* had they been in your hand. The *7* gives you *19*, and a *5* gives you *17*.

Now reverse the situation and take the *7/5*. That makes the *10* and the *deuce* available. The *10* busts you and the *deuce* gives you *14* which has essentially the same value as *12*. That double flip-flop makes a difference, even with

96

up to six decks! Thus, *against a 4 up, if your 12 comes in the form of 10/2, hit!* But stand with any other kind of hard *12*. The two illustrations below tell the story:

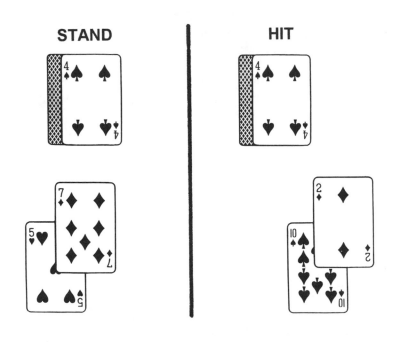

STAND   HIT

BOARD-SENSITIVE HANDS

The second type of borderline hands in blackjack are called *"board-sensitive"* hands. These get a little bit more involved.

You see, the basic strategy assumes that all cards except for the dealer's up-card and the player's starting hand are *equally available*. But in reality, their availability varies

97

as cards are played out. With most hands that doesn't really make a difference. But there are a small handful of situations in blackjack that are so marginal, or *"borderline"* that subtle irregularities right there on the table can actually change the correct decision to some other play. By reacting to those indicators, you can increase your chances just slightly with those hands.

What are the pertinent indicators? Blackjack is basically a game of high and low cards. About 30% of all the cards are *10's*. When you glance around the board at the other players' hands, about 30% of *their* cards should also be *10's*. Take a look at the scenario below:

It's a multi-deck shoe game with all the cards dealt face-up. You are seated to the left. You have *12* against the dealer's *4* up. There are three other players at the table with you and they have all stayed pat. Now it's your turn. Look at the other players' cards. Notice anything unusual? Among six cards there are four *10's*. Is that normal? No, it's not.

98

There should only be two *10's!* With your hand, standing will win just a shade more often than hitting; *if all the other cards are equally available.* You should win 40% of the time by standing because that's how often the dealer will bust with a *4* up; *usually.* But if only a couple of extra *10-cards* have come out as they have here, the dealer will break just a little *less* often. And at the same time if you hit, you will *make* a hand just a little *more* often. Now all of a sudden the percentages are reversed, and you should *hit!* This is what is meant by reacting appropriately to the subtle indicators on the board.

Blackjack's board-sensitive hands for *four* to *six* decks are listed below in their order of frequent appearance.

BOARD-SENSITIVE HANDS
for 4 or 6 DECKS

16 vs. a **10 up**

12 vs. a **4 up**

9 vs. a **2 up**

A/2 vs. a **5 up**

The basic strategy plays for these hands are correct by a very tiny margin. But that's if everything's *exactly normal!* In a four to six deck game, whenever you've been dealt one of these hands, you should take a look around at the board. There may be a dozen face-up cards to be seen in the hands of the other players. But you don't have to see *that* many cards for you to be able to gain useful information. As illustrated on the previous page, there can be as few as six. The following list shows how many *10's* should normally be among the other exposed cards on board.

99

Remember, these are the other cards on board, not including your own or the dealer's up-card. Those have already been factored into the basic strategy.

CARDS ON BOARD	NORMAL No. of 10's
6	2
10	3
13	4

In four to six deck play, if the other players' cards contain just *two* too many *10's,* or *two* too few, that skews the composition of the remaining cards enough to change the correct decision to a different play with these board-sensitive hands, and *only* these hands.

LIGHT BOARD / HEAVY BOARD

When the rest of the board is *missing* two *10's,* the board is said to be *light.* When it contains two *extra 10's,* that's a *heavy* board. For example, with ten exposed cards, a minimum of five *10's (instead of the normal three)* would be required to constitute a *heavy* board. No more than one *10* present among ten cards would constitute a *light* board.

The chart on the next page lists blackjack's board-sensitive hands for 4 to 6 decks along with their standard basic strategy decisions, accompanied by the refined play that should *supersede* the basic strategy *whenever the board is appropriately abnormal.*

HAND	BASIC STRATEGY	BOARD CONDITION	REFINED PLAY
16 vs.10	HIT	LIGHT	**STAND**
12 vs. 4	STAND	HEAVY	**HIT**
9 vs. 2	HIT	LIGHT	**DOUBLE**
A/2 vs. 5	DOUBLE	HEAVY	**HIT**

The presence of a *light* or *heavy* board will also override the strategy rules for *composition-sensitive* hands. For example, suppose you have *12* against a *4* up and your *12* is composed of *10/2*. That normally means you should hit. But if there happens to be a light board out there, you should now **stand!** Those two extra *10's* in the shoe *(missing from the board)* cancel out the reason why you would have taken a hit with your *10/2*. So the proper hierarchy for the play of your hands goes like this:

HIERARCHY of PLAY

3) BASIC STRATEGY *overridden by*
2) HAND COMPOSITION *overridden by*
1) BOARD CONDITION

16 vs. a 10 up: The basic strategy here says to hit. But when the board is *light* you should **stand** *(regardless of hand composition)!* It's not that a *10* is suddenly now "due", but with a couple extra ones lurking somewhere, that's enough to tip the scales in favor of standing.

101

12 vs. a 4 up: Just as with the illustration on page 98, and the explanation in the middle of page 101, your playing decision is subject to change from *stand* to *hit*, or from *hit* to *stand* depending upon the condition of the board. The board-sensitive decision outranks both the basic strategy and the composition-sensitive strategy.

9 vs. a deuce up: In multi-deck play this hand is just a smidge short of being a correct double down. But a *light* board makes you about 1% more likely to catch a *10*. Plus, the dealer is just a shade more likely to be *stiff* (have *12*). This gives you enough of an edge to go ahead and double.

Ace/2 vs. a 5 up: This is just barely a profitable double down in a shoe game. But with a *heavy* board, you've lost your edge and should just take a hit.

In 4 or 6 deck blackjack, there are only four borderline hands because just seeing a few biased cards on the board is not enough to change the composition of the other two to three hundred unnoticed cards very much. Besides that, the board will only be out of balance by two tens about one time out of six or seven, so borderline play is not much of a factor in shoe games. In fact, as stated before this strategy shouldn't even be applied in 8 deck play.

But with single or double deck play, the composition of a half dozen cards on the table can have a much greater effect on the remaining fifty or hundred cards in the deck. Consequently there are more borderline hands to react to. **But the big factor is, the board only has to be *light* or *heavy* by *ONE 10* in order to prompt a different decision!** Because of this, you'll be changing up your play on the following hands about a third of the time.

102

BOARD-SENSITIVE HANDS for
SINGLE or DOUBLE DECK

16 vs. a **10** up
12 vs. a **4** up
11 vs. an **A** up
8 vs. a **6** up
A/8 vs. a **6** up
A/6 vs. a **2** up
10/3 vs. a **2** up

Remember, when playing with one or two decks, if the board contains just *one* extra *10*, or is just *one 10* short of normal that will activate the borderline play. So with a board of six cards, since *two 10's* would be normal, then *one 10* constitutes a *light* board and *three 10's* makes the board *heavy*.

That means you can react to a board that has as few as three cards on it by noticing that it contains either *zero* or *two 10's!* This is important because most single and double deck games are dealt face-down. So before you play your hand, you'll only get to see the other players' hit, split and double down cards, or their busted hands. Let's look at the illustration on the following page:

You are last. All the cards have been dealt face-down. The other players have taken a total of three hits, none of which were *10's*. Assuming you haven't seen their hole cards, that constitutes a light board so you should now **stand** rather than **hit!**

From this, you should be able to see that whenever you're playing at a level where you're reacting to the cards that have been dealt, it pays to sit as close to third base as possible. In that way, you'll be able to eliminate some cards before you play your hand.

The following chart tells you how to play the board-sensitive hands for single and double deck blackjack.

104

HAND	BASIC STRATEGY	BOARD CONDITION	REFINED PLAY
16 vs.10	HIT	LIGHT	**STAND**
12 vs. 4	STAND	HEAVY	**HIT**
11 vs. A	DOUBLE	HEAVY	**HIT**
8 vs. 6	HIT	LIGHT	**DOUBLE**
A/8 vs. 6	STAND	LIGHT	**DOUBLE**
A/6 vs. 2	HIT	LIGHT	**DOUBLE**
10/3 vs. 2	STAND	HEAVY	**HIT**

The first six hands are pretty self-explanatory, but the last hand in the chart, *"10/3 vs. 2"* is somewhat of a special case. It of course means that you have *13* against a deuce up. But your *13* can come a lot of different ways. They are *7/6, 8/5, 9/4,* and four different versions of *10/3* counting the *Jacks, Queens* and *Kings* separately. So four times out of seven, your *13* will have a *10* in it, but the other three times it won't.

This hand is very similar to having *12* against a *4* up. But with *13* against a *deuce*, just its composition alone is not enough to cause you to change your play from the basic strategy*. This hand needs a double-qualifier in order for you to react. First, your *13* must be made up of *10/3.* Then the board must be *heavy.* If both those conditions are present, *hit!* But just follow the basic strategy and stand if you hold any of the other forms of *13, or if the board is normal.*

---

*Actually, when playing with a *single* deck and *only* with a single deck, *10/3* vs. a *deuce* should be hit even if the board is normal. There are also a small number of other hands in single deck play that are

105

sensitive to hand composition, but are not mentioned here because of the growing scarcity of one deck blackjack games. For the most complete rundown I've ever seen of these specifics, see "The Theory of Blackjack", by Peter Griffin.

This chapter on borderline hands contains only the "tip of the iceberg" regarding all the ways you can learn to play your hands more efficiently by gathering additional information. The ones supplied here are those that only require you to notice either the specific cards that compose your hand, or the other cards on the board.

But rest assured that as a card counter, if I were to be dealt any one of these hands and the qualifying conditions were met, *my count would instruct me to make these modified plays.* If you can learn to use this information, then to that minimal extent, *you too would be a card counter.*

How much can playing all the borderline hands help your game? Probably less than a tenth of a percent, even with one or two decks. Think of it as gaining the option to surrender or re-split *Aces.* But even if you never progress beyond the basic strategy and into card counting, you should still be aware that there *are* things you can react to that can occasionally help you out of a tight spot, or enable you to take advantage of a favorable opportunity.

If you choose to learn nothing else about borderline hands, you *should* become familiar with how to play the different forms of *16* against a *10.* It's not hard to do, and you'll find yourself looking at that hand much more often than you'd like to for as long as you play this game.

106

Chapter 6
KEY POINTS

1) For basic strategy players, blackjack is a game of "rote". But beginning with borderline hands, it starts to involve personal analysis.

2) The basic strategy assumes that all cards except for the two that make up your hand and the dealer's up-card are equally available. This is not always so.

3) In determining how to play your cards, the basic strategy only considers "starting hands" such as "10/6". It does not take "built-up" hands into account such as "7/5/4".

4) Some blackjack situations are so marginal that the specific cards which make up your total can alter the correct play from "stand" to "hit", or "hit" to "double down".

5) In other cases, the mere presence of just a few high or low cards on the board can also make it correct to play your hand differently from the basic strategy.

6) By reacting to the "composition" of your hand or by noticing a lop-sided distribution of cards on the board you can slightly increase your chances to win with certain "borderline" hands.

7

the "*High Card /* *Low Card*" *Axiom*

A key ingredient that sets blackjack apart from other casino-banked table games is the fact that the controls are not set back to square one after each bet is settled. If somebody was just dealt two pair in Caribbean stud, it really doesn't make a bit of difference after the deck is shuffled and they start to deal the next hand. The odds against receiving another two pair hand are still, and always will be 20 to 1.

But in blackjack, several hands are dealt between shuffles. This is a major factor to the truly diligent *"21"* player. That's because the odds of being dealt good hands or bad hands vary as the cards are played out.

If you've been around the game of blackjack any length of time at all, I'm sure you've heard it said somewhere that high cards, like *10's* and *Aces* favor the player. Is this just an old piece of gambling folklore, or is there something to it?

108

Well, there's a *lot* to it! *Not only do high cards favor the player, but low cards favor the dealer as well!* Now, some people's response to this statement might be, "Yeah, but when a lot of high cards are left, doesn't the dealer have the same chance of getting a *10* or an *Ace* as the player?" Yes he does; exactly the same chance. But the player can do a lot more with high cards than the dealer can. That's because as pointed out in Chapter 2 *(the House Edge)*, the player and dealer don't really play by quite the same rules. Sure, they're both trying to make *"21"*, but that's where the similarity ends.

As you know, the player may hit or stand at will while the dealer *must* hit *16* or less. But are you aware that the basic strategy player *voluntarily* elects to *stand* on 35% of his stiffs *(12 through16)?* The dealer however, must hit them *all*, even if he already has your *13* beaten with *16!* This makes small cards very useful to the dealer.

Here's a question for you. What's the most valuable card in the deck for the dealer? Congratulations if you said the *"5".* Why? Because a five-spot will turn every dealer's stiff into a made hand. Notice that by catching a *5*, a *12* becomes *17* and a *16* becomes *21*. That's a pretty sweet ending for someone who's *forced* to play Russian roulette! In fact, computer analysis studies have shown that the *5* is the most important card in the entire game, mostly because it bails the dealer out of so many tight spots. The next most useful cards to the dealer are the *4* and then the *6*.

Conversely, only the player receives a $1\frac{1}{2}$ to 1 payoff for his blackjacks which makes those *10's* and *Aces* more valuable to him than they are to the dealer. Also, the player can split up lousy pairs like *Aces* or *8's*. Here again, a high card would come in handy. And finally, the player is

109

usually rooting for a big card when doubling down. In fact, when there are lot of *10's* in the deck, even the insurance bet becomes an advantage to the player. Indeed, most of the options that are exclusively available to the player are enhanced by the presence of high cards.

So what's the most valuable card in the deck for the player? The *9* is a *little* bit of help, but for top honors it's a real close call between the *10* and the *Ace*. The more of these there are, the more times the player will be able to take advantage of his right to double down, split and of course, get paid a bonus on his blackjacks.

SPANISH "21"

As of this writing, a relatively new form of blackjack is beginning to pop up in some casinos. It's called *"Spanish 21"*. It has terrific rules. The player's blackjack beats a dealer's blackjack. A player's *21* beats the dealer's *21*. You can double down on any two, three or four cards. You can surrender half your double bet after you double down if you don't like the card you caught. You can take extra hits to your split *Aces*. And there are some bonuses for special hands like *7-7-7* or a five card *21* among other perks. How can they do this? *They take all the 10-spots out of the deck!* The *Jacks, Queens* and *Kings* remain, thus **the shoe has been depleted of 25% of its *10's*.**

PINOCHLE BLACKJACK

Still need more convincing? Then you owe it to yourself to walk over to the kitchen table and deal yourself some blackjack with a pinochle deck, where the smallest card is a *9*. Take full advantage of all those high cards by splitting *10's* every time the dealer has a *9* showing. Double down with *Ace/9* against a *9* up and always take insurance. Keep score for 40 or 50 hands. It should become obvious what's happening.

You see, with no cards smaller than a *9*, everybody is always dealt a pat hand, except for a pair of Aces. You can never bust *(except by suicide)!* That *was* the dealer's sole advantage; that he always takes your money immediately when you bust, even if he breaks later in the hand himself. With all else being equal, it would now be an even game. Aah, *but all else is not equal!*

Why not? For one thing, the dealer can still bust. How? What about when he has a pair of *Aces?* If *you* have a pair of *Aces*, you get to hit *11* twice by splitting, and the deck is loaded with *10's!* You'll *never* bust and your average finishing hand will be $19^2/3$. But the *dealer* has to hit a soft *12!* Virtually the only way he can *avoid* busting is to catch a *9* in there somewhere.

Besides that, you still get paid $1^1/2$ to 1 on your blackjacks. And now, your blackjacks will come once every $4^1/2$ hands instead of the normal once in 21 hands. And you still can split pairs and double down in those spots where it is to your advantage to do so.

Plus, now the insurance wager favors the player instead of the house! Why? Because you'll win two out of every three insurance bets collecting 2 units for each win, and losing 1 unit for your loss. And the dealer will have an *Ace* up once every 6 hands instead of one time in 13. With a pinochle deck, blackjack isn't even close! And the closer a blackjack deck gets to being a pinochle deck, the more it favors the player. *Am I making sense?*

111

Still have your doubts about high cards in blackjack? Okay, then you're a prime candidate for the ultimate acid test. How about a nice private game of "Strip-Blackjack" with your girlfriend using a pinochle deck? You be the big, bad "invincible" dealer; let her be the "defenseless" little player. But wear a lot of extra clothes; you're going to need them!

Okay, so maybe high cards do help the player. So what? Well, the obvious thing would be to bet more when a lot of high cards are left in the deck, or shoe. In a 6 deck game the distribution of high and low cards remains nearly normal about 70% of the time. During these stretches, the house enjoys an edge of about $1/2$%. Another 15% of the time, there are a lot of little cards left and the house advantage swells to an average of about $2^1/2$%. During the remaining 15% of the time, there is a surplus of high cards and the *player* has an advantage averaging about $1^1/2$%.

With a single deck, the shifting percentages are more dramatic. The player will have the advantage on the next hand about one-third of the time, and by a larger margin. Why is this? Since the player only has an edge when the composition of remaining cards gets out of kilter, the fewer cards that are involved, the more easily it can happen.

Picture it this way. Let's say you were going to flip three coins in the air, and in order to win they had to come down at least two-thirds heads. This would happen successfully 50% of the time. But if you threw 30 coins into the air and still needed two-thirds heads, you'd only get 20 or more heads 5% of the time. With so many more coins falling, the distribution of heads and tails would hang closer to 50-50. *This is how the house begins to insulate itself from card counters when they use multi-deck shoes.*

112

Anyway, be it one deck or six, by staying aware of the condition of the remaining pack, card counters can bet more when they have the advantage, and less the rest of the time. If you can bet more money when you have the advantage than you did all the rest of the times that you were at a disadvantage, *then you become the overall favorite in the game!*

Don't think for a second that this is an easy task. Pay close attention to the small edges we're working with here. Lot's of rookie card counters think when a strong count has them betting it up, they have a license to steal. This is far from true. You'll never get to play with cards nearly as "rich" as a pinochle deck.

In multi-deck shoe games, you'll seldom have more than a 51% chance to win that big bet you've just made. Sometimes you'll count through four shoes waiting to find an opportunity to put some real money out there, and when it finally comes you'll lose five or six big bets in a row. *Put that together with any mistakes you may have made, throw in a couple of tips for the dealer and it's a mighty tough way to make some easy money!*

This is the nature of gambling. You'll have a tiny edge, but it's no guarantee that you'll win. *Still, keeping track of at least some of the cards that have been dealt is superior to playing straight basic strategy by simple virtue of having a modest edge on your larger bets.*

If you're already fluent with the complete basic strategy and want more from blackjack, your next logical step would be to learn how to track a few *key* cards to give you an idea when you have the advantage. A recreational, entry level card tracking system, the *"Key Card Count"* is thoroughly illustrated in Chapter 8 for just that purpose.

113

Chapter 7
KEY POINTS

1) A key ingredient that makes blackjack mathematically beatable is that the controls are not set back to square one by shuffling after each hand is played.

2) Since the rules are somewhat different for the player than the dealer, high cards help the player win money, and low cards help the dealer.

3) By keeping track of when the remaining cards are predominantly high, the player can gain an edge if he bets more at those times.

4) The fact that high cards help the player is evidenced by the development of new blackjack games with super-loose rules and some of the 10's removed from the pack.

5) The advantage that high cards afford the player can be easily demonstrated simply by playing blackjack for a short while with a pinochle deck, where the smallest card is a 9.

SECTION D

Keeping Track of the Cards

8

the Key Card Count

If you've learned everything that's been presented in this manual thus far, you'll be playing a tough enough game of blackjack that you should win about 45% of your three to four hour playing sessions. That by itself is better than your chances in practically any other casino-banked game.

But now it's time for a small dose of grim reality. In spite of all the astute fine points you may learn to use, and no matter how you may couple them with a lot of other *nonsense*, such as *progressive betting schemes, quitting when you're ahead*, etc. *you still won't be able to gain the upper hand in this game unless you can learn to keep track of at least some of the cards that have been played!*

This is the one loophole in casino-banked table games. Since the player is actually the favorite in blackjack an average of about one hand in five, he can chip away at that final morsel of disadvantage by betting more at those times. *It's the only way to implement a system of betting that will actually tend to win the larger bets and lose the smaller ones!* In that respect:

116

CARD COUNTING IS REALITY'S ANSWER TO PROGRESSIVE BETTING SYSTEMS!

"But doesn't keeping track of the cards require a tremendous memory?" you may ask. No, it doesn't! Allow me to explain why.

"HOW MUCH IS MY WALLET WORTH?"

Suppose I were to hand you my wallet and ask you how much money was in it. After counting up all the $1, $5, $10 and $20 bills, you gave it back to me and confidently announced, *"Two hundred thirty-seven dollars"*. If I then asked you how many of each bill denomination there were, you probably wouldn't have any idea. But you would still know the value of the contents of my wallet, wouldn't you?

Well, that's how card counting works. You really don't **remember** any cards at all. You merely **count** them. And that count tells you the value of the contents of the remaining shoe or deck.

When I count cards, I really don't have the foggiest recollection of how many *Jacks*, or *Aces* or *5's* I may have seen. But I did count them as they went by, and I have a running total in my head at all times. That total tells me what I need to know about the remaining cards.

Card counting systems have been around for a long time. In general, they are not a recreational tool. Most fully structured card counts keep track of about 80% of all the cards that have been played. To master one of these systems requires at least scores, if not hundreds of hours of practice. There are very, very few blackjack players who are both

117

willing and able to persevere to that level of expertise with a full scale card count.

There is however, an intermediate step between basic strategy and a full blown card counting system. It's called the *Key Card Count*. It's ideal for the serious blackjack player who wishes to take his game up a notch, but still wants to keep things at a recreational level. According to my computer simulation runs involving millions of hands, using it accurately will improve the performance of a basic strategy player by just about $3/4\%$. That means in a typical multi-deck game, the Key Card Count will give you about a $1/4\%$ edge over the house.

Here's how the Key Card Count works. We already know that in blackjack, some cards affect the odds of the game more than others. So if you wanted to keep track of just a few cards in the deck, you would of course choose the most important ones. The two most significant *low* cards in blackjack are the *4* and the *5*. Among *high* cards, the *10's* and *Aces* are critical. Cards like the *2, 7* and *9* are much less important.

The Key Card Count monitors just 14 of the most important cards in each 52 card deck to give you a rough idea where the advantage lies during the course of the game. In addition, it has some simplifications built into it to make it more "user friendly" at the expense of minimal accuracy. A graphic showing the Key Card Count is depicted below:

The Key Card Count

CARD RANK

2	3	4	5	6	7	8	9	10	J	Q	K	redA	blkA
0	0	+1	+1	0	0	0	0	-1	0	0	0	0	-1

Of course the *Jack, Queen* and *King* are every bit as important as the *10-spot*. But the Key Card Count is a *"mini"* card tracking system designed to improve the performance of the recreational player. Among the *10-count* cards, the *10-spot* was chosen for it's distinctly different appearance than the *picture cards*. By monitoring the distribution of these key cards, you will be aware of roughly 2/3 of the occasions that you have the advantage on the next hand.

It is not recommended that you play against 8 decks while tracking the cards. Finding an adequate imbalance in the high-low composition of the remaining cards occurs infrequently enough with 4 or 6 decks as it is. *The more decks in play, the less often the house will be dealing hands with a composition of cards that favors the player.*

THE COUNTING PROCESS

When counting cards, you must always begin off the top of a *fresh* deck, or shoe. If you come in during the middle of a deal, you won't know what's been played up to this point. If you're playing against a single deck, begin your count before you see the first card with the number **"18"** in your mind. With two decks, you'll begin the count at **"16"**. With a four deck shoe, start off at **"12"**, and with six decks, begin at **"8"**. This is called your *running count.*

Now, every time a **4** or a **5** comes out, add one point to your total. And with each **10** or **black Ace** that is dealt, subtract one point from your total. Just ignore any *red Aces!* *Got that?*

119

Okay, let's practice counting a few cards. You've just taken a seat at a table where they're dealing from a six deck shoe. The dealer is shuffling, so clear your mind and pre-load your count by putting the number **"8"** in your head. Place your minimum bet *(because the house always has the advantage on the first hand off the top of a fresh shoe)*. There are two other players at the table with you. Here comes the first hand:

The cards you count here are the *10*, the *5* and the *4*. *Ignore all the other ones even though they may matter.* They are not within the scope of the Key Card system. Your running count would now be **"9"**. If the next round of cards was;

you would count both *10's,* the *Ace* of clubs and the *4* to put your running count at **"7"**. Okay now, *you* tell *me;* after all the cards below came out on the next couple of hands, what would your running count be?

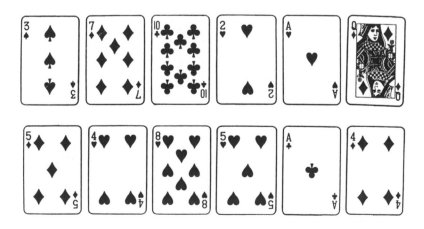

121

Look carefully. If you didn't get a count of "9", go back and check again. When you're playing, be sure to notice every card that gets turned up. Don't worry about missing the burn card at the beginning of the deal, or one that may get burned while the dealers are switched at your table. It's not enough to make a significant difference. Any burned card is in the same category as all those behind the plastic cut-off card; *unknown* and theoretically available.

PRACTICE, PRACTICE, PRACTICE

Practice counting with a single deck by turning the cards over one at a time, in as rapid succession as you can without making a mistake. For practicing, start off your count at **"18"**. When you have one card left, *stop! Can you name the category of the last card?* There are 3 choices:

A) a *4* or *5*
B) a *10-spot* or *black Ace*
C) a *"non-counter"*

Since you've been counting eight low cards and only six high cards, the running count should rise by two points to **"20"** after you get through a complete deck. So, if your count with one card left is **"19"**, then the last card should be a *4* or *5*. If your count is **"21"**, the last card is a *10* or *black Ace*. And if your count is already **"20"**, then the final card is a *"no-counter"*. When you can count down a 52 card deck comfortably and accurately *within 30 seconds*, you're ready for casino action.

Wondering why you're only counting the *black Aces* and not the red ones? Good question! Typically, full blown counting systems have *balanced* card counts. That is, you count the same number of high cards as low cards and begin

122

your count at "0". With those, you are required to divide the running count by the number of decks that remain to find out how strong or weak the *high-low ratio* of unplayed cards has become. That is referred to as the *"true count"*.

With the *unbalanced* Key Card scheme, you just keep counting and if the *running count* ever reaches **"20"**, it's time to raise your bet, *with any number of cards remaining! The high-low ratio, or "true count" has been automatically calibrated to be accurate at this particular point!* With a running count of **"20"** you will usually have about a 1/2% advantage no matter if there are four decks remaining or just one deck. The further above **"20"** the running count climbs, the bigger favorite you are and the more you should bet. This streamlining feature will make it easier for you to recognize when you have the edge.

The following table describes what would be an *ideal* betting strategy for the Key Card Count:

BETTING STRATEGY

| RUNNING | BET SIZE | |
COUNT	1 or 2 Decks	4 or 6 Decks
19 or less	1 unit	1 unit
20	2 units	3 units
21	4 units	----
22	6 units	6 units
23	----	8 units
24	----	12 units

So much for ideals! The reality is, with 1 or 2 decks, your running count will bounce back and forth, above and below **"20"** so quickly that you will probably not

123

be able to bet in direct accordance with the table. If you did, you're "wild" betting would attract undesirable attention from the pit. It would be good policy to never more than double your last bet, no matter how sharply the count may rise. It's easiest to do this when you've won the last hand, by letting your winnings ride.

In single deck play, you should begin òff the top of each deck with a 2 unit wager, then drop to 1 unit if the count is still below "20" at the start of the second hand. In that way, it will be easier to get to the larger bets without such a drastic change in wager size. Even at that, you may have extreme difficulty getting down a 6 unit bet without the dealer shuffling abruptly. *This is something you must avoid!* It would be much better to have 4 units riding on a "24" count hand than to get it shuffled away. *You* will have to be the judge of how much betting latitude you can get away with in these games. That's where the *art* of the game comes into play. And mind you, it's all for the benefit of being able eke out the most trivial advantage, which by the way, your floorman has no intention of letting you do.

In 4 or 6 deck play, everything will move much more gradually. Besides that, pit crews are less paranoid about card counters when multiple decks are used. Consequently, you should have no trouble betting in direct accordance with the count. Your "20+" counts may only occur once every 3 or 4 shoes and will usually come nearer the end of the shoe. You need such a wider spread in your betting units when playing the shoe games because you won't have the advantage very often. When you do, you need to get more money on the table than you risked through all those waiting bets. This of course will lead to greater volatility in your results. In a three or four hour playing session, you'll generally find that the outcome of a few hundred hands of blackjack depended upon how you did with maybe two dozen assorted large bets.

In all cases, it's important to count accurately all the way through so that you'll never be making multi-unit bets when the count is below **"20"** and you actually have a disadvantage. On average, you should find when the shuffle occurs that the running count will be about **"17"** if the are 1¹/₂ decks left.

Playing the
"ADVANTAGE STRATEGY"

When the running count reaches **"20"**, there is a large enough surplus of *10's* and *Aces*, and a shortage of *4's* and *5's* in the unplayed cards to make the player a money favorite on the next hand. That's why you should raise your bet. *Also, at these times some hands could be played more productively than by simply following the basic strategy.*

The basic strategy is the player's blackjack bible. About 95% of the time it's the right way to go. But the basic strategy has determined the right play based on the assumption that all cards are equally available. When the running count is **"20"** or higher, all cards are *not* equally available! Some hands only require a modest shift in the high-low strength of the remaining cards to render a different play the superior choice.

125

When your count reaches **"20"** or above, the following twelve hands should be played according to the *"Advantage Strategy"* rather than the basic strategy *or any other strategy based on hand or board composition!* It is called the Advantage Strategy because this will be your playing mode when you have the advantage. *This will be the most efficient way to play these twelve hands at that time.*

ADVANTAGE STRATEGY HANDS

HAND	Basic Strategy	ADVANTAGE STRATEGY
8 vs. 6 up	hit	DOUBLE
9 vs. 2 up	hit	DOUBLE
11 vs. Ace	hit	DOUBLE
12 vs. 3 up	hit	STAND
12 vs. 4 up	stand	STAND
10/3 vs. 2 up	stand	STAND
16 vs. 10 up	hit	STAND
A2 vs. 5 up	double	DOUBLE
A6 vs. 2 up	hit	DOUBLE
A7 vs. 2 up	stand	DOUBLE
A8 vs. 5 up	stand	DOUBLE
A8 vs. 6 up	stand	DOUBLE

Notice that a few of the plays already coincide with the basic strategy. These are hands that are part of the strategy for *Borderline Hands.* The point is:

When the count is "20" or greater, it won't matter how many decks you're playing with, which particular cards compose your hand or what cards are on the board!

The deck condition will be such that *all* of these hands should be played according to the Advantage Strategy, whether that violates the basic strategy or any other!

TAKING INSURANCE

By now you know that Insurance is nothing more than a catchy side bet invented by the casino to make more money for the house. How does the house do this? They do it the same way they make money when they pay you 2 to 1 odds on column #1 at the roulette table when it's really 2¹/₆ to 1 against a number in column #1 coming up. They make money the same way at the craps table by paying 9 to 5 odds for a place bet on the 10, when the true odds are 2 to 1 against making that 10. They're always paying you shorter odds than the true odds against winning your bet.

Whenever you take Insurance at the blackjack table, you're simply betting that the dealer has a *10* in the hole, and the house will pay you 2 to 1 odds on your Insurance bet if she does. But the true odds against the dealer having that *10* in the hole are **usually** 2¹/₄ to 1.

USUALLY is the key word here! You see, hitting column #1 in roulette is **always** a 2¹/₆ to 1 shot. Making a 10 in craps is **always** 2 to 1 against. But the dealer having a *10* underneath her *Ace* is **usually** 2¹/₄ to 1! It all depends upon how many *10's* are left in the unplayed cards! *Fact is, sometimes the odds are 2³/₄ to 1, and sometimes they are 1³/₄ to 1.* Whenever the odds are below 2 to 1, the player has the edge on the Insurance bet instead of the house!

In 4 to 6 deck shoe games, on average, when your Key Card count is **"25"**, the odds against the dealer having a *10* in the hole will be under 2 to 1. With 1 or 2 decks, this usually occurs at a count of **"23"**. So whenever your running count is **"25"** or higher in shoe games, or at least **"23"** in single or double deck play, *Take Insurance!*

127

Why? Because you'll win more than $^1/_3$ of those bets, and that puts you on the right side of *the basic principle of profitable gambling.* Remember, it doesn't matter what your hand is. You're betting on something else. You'll win or lose your hand just the same. The two bets are not the slightest bit related. You take Insurance at a specified count because you have uncovered an advantageous bet. You are not trying to hedge the bet on your hand.

With the Key Card Count, your running count will not reach **"25"** very often because you're not tracking that many *10-count* cards. With some of the more structured card counts, you would be able to uncover a greater number of advantageous insurance betting opportunities.

So remember, you now have three things to pay attention to that as a basic strategy player, you never had to think about. They are printed out for you in two complete tables on these next two pages:

The Complete
KEY CARD COUNT STRATEGY
(for 1 or 2 Decks)

RUNNING COUNT	BETTING STRATEGY	PLAYING STRATEGY
thru 19	1 or 2 units	Basic
20	2 units	Advantage
21	4 units	Advantage
22	6 units	Advantage
23+	6 units	Advantage + Insurance

The Complete
KEY CARD COUNT STRATEGY
(for 4 or 6 Decks)

RUNNING COUNT	BETTING STRATEGY	PLAYING STRATEGY
thru 19	1 unit	Basic
20	3 units	Advantage
22	6 units	Advantage
23	8 units	Advantage
24	12 units	Advantage
25+	12 units	Advantage + Insurance

For sizing your bets, use these tables as an *ideal* benchmark. But remember that with fewer decks you'll need to moderate your actual wagers so as not to attract attention.

Chapter 8
KEY POINTS

1) Playing the correct basic strategy will only *minimize* the casino's edge over a player at blackjack. Also, playing all the borderline hands appropriately will further trim that house advantage.

2) In order to actually gain the upper hand however, the player *must* learn to keep track of at least a few *key* cards.

3) Card counting does not require a photographic memory since you don't actually remember any cards at all. You merely count them.

4) Most full-fledged counting systems track about 80% of the cards. They require a great deal of concentration, and practice in order to be used effectively.

5) The Key Card Count is a greatly simplified, *introductory* counting system that is less effective than a full scale card count, but better than just playing the basic strategy.

6) You keep track of the cards not only to bet more when you have the advantage. In some cases, your count will tell you to play your hand differently from the basic strategy as well.

7) There are also situations where your count will point out that it is to your advantage to take insurance.

9

the **Black Ace Count**

The Key Card Count is a *beginner level* introduction to the basic concepts of card counting. It will train you to pay attention to the things that you *must* in order to even have a chance to win at blackjack over the long haul. With it, you can still play a relatively relaxed game of "21", while gaining useful information as to sizing your next wager, and in some cases how to play your hand. In tracking just over one-fourth of the cards in the deck, the Key Card Count is 65% efficient at detecting when the player has the edge.

For many of you, the Key Card Count will be more than enough to keep you busy. But after a while, if you find yourself comfortable with juggling numbers in your head, you may want to do a better job of analyzing the condition of the unplayed cards. The good news here is that the Key Card Count is *"expandable."* In fact, it is actually an abbreviated version of something called *"the Black Ace Count"*. That term, as you may have noticed arises from the fact that the only *Aces* you count are the black ones.

131

When you're ready to step up to *"intermediate card counting"*, the *Black Ace Count* should be a fairly smooth transition for you. It carries an 86% efficiency rating for monitoring where the advantage lies. In computer simulation runs, it improved the player's performance by about 1% over the basic strategy in typical blackjack games, providing him with an overall advantage of $1/2$% or more.

Mind you, these are results achieved by a computer that never mis-counts a card, never misplays a hand and never absorbs the cost of tipping a dealer. Also, the computer was never subjected to a range of countermeasures that any casino is likely to impose upon a suspected counter, particularly in 1 and 2 deck games. Nevertheless, with the Black Ace Count you do have a meaningful, although risky and delicate mathematical edge, if you can implement all of it successfully.

According to computer studies, the four most important *low* cards in the game of blackjack are the *3, 4, 5* and *6*. The Black Ace Count monitors the dispersion of those low cards along with the *black Aces* and all the *face-cards* (but not the *10-spot)*. The following graphic lays it all out for you:

The Black Ace Count

			CARD		RANK								
2	3	4	5	6	7	8	9	10	J	Q	K	red A	blk A
0	+1	+1	+1	+1	0	0	0	0	-1	-1	-1	0	-1

For quick and easy recognition, the *face-cards* have replaced the *10-spot*. The Black Ace Count will keep you

132

considerably busier than before. You will be adjusting your running count on 4 out of every 7 cards that come out. You should still practice counting the same way, and you still need to be able to count down a single deck in 30 seconds.

You will begin your count at all the same pre-set numbers as with the Key Card Count, such as starting off a six deck shoe with a running count of **"8"**. And just as before, you will increase your bet and kick in the *Advantage Playing Strategy* at a count of **"20"**. But since you're tracking more cards, it will happen a bit more often. That's because the Black Ace Count will sense some positive deck situations that the Key Card Count missed. Also, since you'll be tracking the supply of *10's* a lot more accurately, you'll be finding more instances where you should take Insurance. With one or two decks, take Insurance at a count of **"22"** or higher. In shoe games, begin insuring at **"23"**. The following two strategy tables will explain it all:

The Complete
BLACK ACE COUNT STRATEGY
(for 1 or 2 Decks)

RUNNING COUNT	BETTING STRATEGY	PLAYING STRATEGY
thru 19	1 or 2 units	Basic
20	2 or 3 units	Advantage
21	4 units	Advantage
22+	6 units	Advantage + Insurance

The Complete
BLACK ACE COUNT STRATEGY
(for 4 or 6 Decks)

RUNNING COUNT	BETTING STRATEGY	PLAYING STRATEGY
thru 19	1 unit	Basic
20	3 units	Advantage
22	6 units	Advantage
23	8 units	Advantage + Insurance
24+	12 units	Advantage + Insurance

Now for all this work, just how big an edge is $1/2\%$ anyway? Well, it's just as big *(or small)* as that $1/2\%$ *disadvantage* that a basic strategy player has! At $20 per hand, if you played 1000 hands *(about 12 hours worth)* of perfect basic strategy blackjack in a typical multi-deck game, you'd wind up losing $110 if the cards broke perfectly normal. With a $1/2\%$ *edge,* you'd win the same $110. **But that's if the cards broke normally!** And you couldn't do it by betting $20 on every hand. Instead, you'd have to vary your bets from $10 to $120 with the count *(which would average out to about $20 per hand).* This erratic betting pattern while necessary, lends greater volatility to a card counter's expectation. In fact it wouldn't take much good or bad luck to win $1000 or lose $800. Remember, this is *gambling.*

134

UP-GRADING the
BLACK ACE COUNT

Some players who had been using the Black Ace Count for a while have later expressed anxiety over not counting *all* the *10's*. This is a reasonable concern. It depends upon how fully you wish to monitor the composition of the unplayed cards. The Black Ace Count is an *intermediate* card count of modest complexity that is nevertheless effective enough to give you a small mathematical edge in blackjack. There's not much beyond it that could still be considered recreational.

Certainly, card counting systems with greater accuracy are available. But more accuracy requires more work. When I play, I count every card except the *8*. It's very accurate, but if you're not comfortable doing that, then it will only get you into trouble.

However, if you find that you've been handling the Black Ace Count with room to spare, there is one more step you can take to raise your performance another notch without stepping over into a full blown "pro-type" counting system. That would be to include the *10-spot* in the card count along with the *deuce* on the low side. With that up-grade, you'll be tracking about 3/4 of the cards and your deck analysis will be 93% efficient for betting purposes. A graphic of the *Up-graded* Black Ace Count is shown below.

the Up-Graded Black Ace Count

CARD   RANK

2	3	4	5	6	7	8	9	10	J	Q	K	red_A	blk_A
+1	+1	+1	+1	+1	0	0	0	-1	-1	-1	-1	0	-1

135

This will boost your overall performance about another 0.1%, producing an overall advantage of fully ²/³% in typical multi-deck games *(with a 1 to 12 betting spread).* The Up-Graded Black Ace Count yields about 85% of all that it's possible to gain with some of the most complicated count systems that exist today. Your starting counts for the different numbers of decks will all remain the same. You will still have about ¹/₂% advantage in most games when your running count reaches **"20"**, but it will be determined with greater accuracy. You should still increase your bet and switch to the *Advantage Strategy* at that same point. You'll find that counting down a single deck in 30 seconds will be a greater challenge, but it remains a requirement.

Also, due to the improved precision of the count, your betting schedule will be slightly revised with multiple decks. The two following tables will outline the complete *ideal* playing and betting strategy for the *Up-Graded Black Ace Count.*

the UP-GRADED
BLACK ACE COUNT STRATEGY
(for 1 or 2 Decks)

RUNNING COUNT	BETTING STRATEGY	PLAYING STRATEGY
thru 19	1 or 2 units	Basic
20	2 or 3 units	Advantage
21	4 units	Advantage
22+	6 units	Advantage + Insurance

136

the UP-GRADED
BLACK ACE COUNT STRATEGY
(for 4 or 6 Decks)

RUNNING COUNT	BETTING STRATEGY	PLAYING STRATEGY
thru 19	1 unit	Basic
20	3 units	Advantage
22	4 units	Advantage
23	6 units	Advantage + Insurance
24	8 units	Advantage + Insurance
25+	12 units	Advantage + Insurance

The Up-Graded Black Ace Count is about as sophisticated as you would care to get with *intermediate* level card counting. In Chapter 11 of this book, *The Mentor Count;* a high performance *advanced* level count system for super-serious blackjack enthusiasts is presented in detail.

But first you should read Chapter 10, the *Art and Science of skillful Play.* Is describes an entire host of tactical and "image" traits that you must develop in order to play *any* count system unimpeded by casino pit personnel.

Chapter 9
KEY POINTS

1) The Black Ace Count is an intermediate level card counting system. It is of the same breed as the Key Card Count but tracks an additional 30% of the cards, thus making it roughly twice as effective.

2) Used accurately, the Black Ace Count will yield about a 1/2% long range mathematical advantage over the house in a typical multi-deck blackjack game (not counting dealer's tips, or casino countermeasures).

3) The Key Card Count and the Black Ace Count use nearly identical betting and playing strategies, making the uphill transition a smooth one.

4) The Black Ace Count can be up-graded further by adding another high and low card to the count, making it still more effective.

10

the Art *and* Science
of Skillful Play

With the proper playing strategy and a reasonably capable count system like the Black Ace Count, you are mathematically equipped to beat the game of blackjack, albeit by a very modest margin. But winning at casino blackjack is a two step process. First you must learn the *science* of how to beat the game. Then you have to learn the *art* of how to beat the house.

The *first* part is no piece of cake. Most players who try, never really quite get the hang of counting cards. But the *second* part is what stops all but the very most dedicated and diligent blackjack buffs!

SUCCEEDING AT THIS GAME WILL REQUIRE NO LESS EFFORT AND FORTITUDE THAN BECOMING A PAR GOLFER OR A 200 BOWLER.

139

It's one thing to understand what makes blackjack tick and set your mind to mastering a winning count system. That's the *scientific* part. You can learn a lot of scientific things from books. But if counting cards is all you ever learn, you've only armed yourself with enough knowledge to land in a world of trouble! That's because, *all the technical studying in the world won't teach you the art of how to be the mouse that sneaks the cheese out from under the cat's nose without his realizing you were capable of taking it!* That only comes with perseverance and seasoning. A successful blackjack player has to be part *scholar* and part *street hustler.* Just knowing a winning count system is not enough!

Once you become thoroughly proficient at counting cards and playing your hands correctly, there are several other tangible skills that must also become an integral part of your blackjack repertoire. Most of them are described below.

PLAYABLE RULES

First and foremost, not all blackjack games are beatable. The biggest initial basic strategy disadvantage you can probably afford to start out with would be about 0.7% with one or two decks, and 0.5% with four or six decks. Eight decks would be a waste of time under the majority of circumstances. Use the *"Rule Variations"* table from Chapter 5 in this book to evaluate each particular game available to you.

Recognize however, that some rules affect the card counter more than the basic strategy player and vise-versa.

140

Surrender for example is more valuable to a card counter due to his increased likelihood of being dealt *15* or *16* against a *10* up when he has a big bet out there. That's because these starting hands are usually comprised of two *10's* and only one *non-10*. Plus, a fully structured count system *(described in the next chapter)* will tell the counter when it's proper to surrender some other hands such as *14* against a *10*, or *15* against a *9*. These occasions too, will only occur when the player has a large bet up. My own computer simulations indicate that surrender is worth about 0.15% to the card counter in multi-deck play.

On the other hand, a rule that hurts the typical player more than a card counter is the *"dealer hits soft 17"* rule. That's because when the counter has his bigger bets riding and the dealer turns up a *soft 17*, there aren't as many small cards available for the dealer to improve his hand. Here again, figure a penalty of about 0.15% for a card counter if the dealer hits a *soft 17*.

DECK PENETRATION

This is a huge factor in obtaining an edge for the card counter. The term "deck penetration" defines how far the deck is dealt out before the shuffle occurs. With a six deck shoe, if they cut off the last two decks, I'd find another table or another casino. A 1$\frac{1}{2}$ deck cutoff is the most I'll generally tolerate in a six deck game. You can often find better than that if you shop table to table. With four decks, a one deck cut-off is usually pretty standard.

The following should give you an idea of just how critical the degree of deck penetration can be. Using the

Mentor Count, *(an advanced card count which follows in the next chapter)* I ran a computer simulation of 75 million hands of blackjack.. The conditions were; six decks, hit on *soft 17*, double on any two starting cards including after splits and a 1 to 16 betting spread. The basic strategy disadvantage for the player was 0.65%. *The only variable in the simulation was the shuffle point.* I started with a two deck cut-off, and after 25 million hands changed to a 1¹/₂ deck shuffle point, then finally to a one deck cutoff. The results for each 25 million hands, are listed below:

CUT-OFF POINT	PLAYER RESULT
2 DECKS	+0.5%
1¹/₂ DECKS	+0.9%
1 DECK	+1.2%

As you can see, even with a powerful tool like the Mentor Count, a two deck cut-off simply kills you! To play in a shoe game with these rules, you absolutely need above average penetration!

In double deck play, some dealers are nice enough to deal out the first 1¹/₂ decks. That would be excellent! In other houses they may insert the cut card midway through the pack, cutting off the last deck. Those are the games you want to avoid. An acceptable cut-off for double deck play is when the cut card is placed about two-thirds of a deck *(one-third of the pack)* from the bottom.

Deck penetration in single deck play is very dependent upon how crowded the tables are. It will be virtually impossible to get adequate penetration at a jammed up table. *Playing with one deck, you absolutely must get a third hand in before the shuffle!* Let that be your barometer. This will seldom occur with more than three players in action.

NUMBER of PLAYERS

Playing at a full table is undesirable to the card counter for two reasons. The most important one is, since you theoretically have an edge you won't be implementing that edge unless you're playing! At a full table you spend a lot of time watching other people play blackjack. The speed at which the hands are dealt varies *dramatically* with the number of players at the table. How many hands you play in an hour's time will also vary with the speed of each dealer, how many decks are in play and whether automatic shufflers are used. But in general the following chart will be fairly accurate.

PLAYERS AT THE TABLE	HANDS PER HOUR
7	55
6	65
5	75
4	90
3	110
2	150
1	230

If you're heads up *(alone)* with the dealer for fifteen minutes, you can actually get in an hour's worth of "full

143

table" blackjack play! This alone is good cause to avoid crowded tables. But there is another lesser reason why you'd like to be as isolated with the dealer as possible. As a counter, in order to acquire an advantage you need to play against deck compositions that have become skewed *(to the high side)*. This can never happen until some cards are removed from play. The more cards that are removed, the more likely this is to occur and the more skewed the remaining cards will become!

Suppose you were playing double deck blackjack and the dealer consistently placed the plastic cut card 40 cards from the bottom of the pack. At a *full table* you would usually be dealt only *three rounds* before the shuffle. One third of your bets would be placed against a full pack *(where you always have a disadvantage)*. When you made your first bet, there will have been no cards removed. When you size your bet for the second and third hands, a total of about 22 and 44 cards will have played out, respectively. At the completion of the third hand, the shuffle will come. Each of those three times you place your bet, the *average* number of cards in the remaining pack will be about 82.

But if it were a *three handed* game you would get in *six or seven hands* between shuffles! Only about 15% of your bets will be made off the top of the pack. And across all six or seven hands, an average of about 77 cards will be left in the pack at the time you size each wager.

PLAYING IN A SHORTER-HANDED GAME HAS THE EFFECT OF ACQUIRING DEEPER OVERALL DECK PENETRATION!

The difference is not always this significant, but you do tend to play against fewer remaining cards at emptier tables! In shoe games *(four or more decks)*, the difference is less important. That's because proportionally speaking, there is a bigger difference between 77 and 82 cards than there is between 200 and 205 *(about average for six deck play)*.

In the following table, the Mentor Count was used to play single deck and six deck blackjack, first heads up *(alone)* with the dealer, and then five-handed. The same rules were in force as with the deck penetration experiment back on page 142. The betting spread remained "1 to 16" for the six deck game and the cut-off point was $1^1/2$ decks. The single deck run used a "1 to 3" betting spread and no hand was dealt with fewer than 22 cards remaining.

DECKS	PLAYERS	RESULT
1	1	+.95%
1	5	+.75%
6	1	+.9%
6	5	+.8%

Here you can see that the fewer the decks, the more important it becomes that the table is not crowded. Now consider that heads up, you'll get in three times as many hands in a given period of time and it becomes obvious that the number of players is a serious factor. Once again, *three players is about maximum for single deck play. Four players is tolerable with two or more decks.*

145

BETTING SPREAD

With blackjack, even an expert player is an underdog in the game the majority of the time. Except for rare cases where the rules are superb and the decks are very few, the card counter only has the advantage when there is a surplus of high cards remaining. During these advantageous periods he basically must put more money in action than he did all the rest of the time in order to become a worthwhile mathematical favorite in the overall game.

Don't think just because you're increasing your bets when the count rises that you automatically have the overall edge. If you're able to use a 1 to 4 betting spread in a typical *single* deck game, yes, you'll have the best of it. That's because the high/low proportion of remaining cards ranges wildly when there were only 52 cards to begin with! Your opportunities to make those three and four unit wagers will arise very frequently. But that same spread just won't get it done with a *312 card shoe!*

The six deck game is slow and dull by card counting standards. That is, you'll be counting and waiting to raise your bets, sometimes for several shoes running. Mathematically, all that time represents lost money because you'll have the short end of the stick pretty much throughout. When a solid positive count finally comes along, you're going to have to get some serious money out there to compensate for the drought. About a 1 to 10 spread would be the minimum that will get the job done here.

The good news about four and six deck shoes is, the count usually rises so gradually that you'll seldom have trouble betting in direct proportion to it. Besides that, pit crews are pretty tolerant of wide betting spreads in shoe

146

games. They are of the opinion that multi-deck games, particularly six or more decks are pretty tough to beat, *and they are right!*

Single and double deck blackjack on the other hand is a much spunkier game. You'll often find your count indicating a single unit bet on one hand, a six unit wager on the next and a single on the hand after that! Unfortunately, you won't be able to change your bet sizes that abruptly. Pit crews in these games are ever-vigilant for signs of card counters, *and that would be a dead giveaway!*

With one deck, a "2/1/4" betting spread may be about the best you'll be able to use over an extended period of time; perhaps even 2/1/3! That means starting off each new deck with a two unit bet, then either cutting back or increasing on the next hand according to the count. Many times you won't even get to double your bet without causing a shuffle up unless you've won the last hand and have let both bets ride. You'll need good rules if you're forced to keep your betting this flat; probably no worse than -0.2% *(basic strategy).* If you're 20 cards into the deck, have lost your last two unit wager and the count calls for a three or four unit bet on the next hand but you fear the dealer will shuffle, *then just bet another two units!*

YOU POSITIVELY MUST AVOID SHUFFLE-UPS!

If you don't, you'll be getting all the negative decks and neutral decks to play with, but not the positive ones. The distribution of cards you will be playing against will have been artificially altered to favor the house. In effect, *it will be like playing with a deck stripped of some of its high cards!*

147

At the same time, being pressured into making nearly flat bets is not a good situation either. Single deck play requires more art than any other "21" game. Until you're really comfortable playing cat and mouse with the pit crew, you may be better off in two and four deck games. Six deck blackjack is a last resort.

Two deck "21" is my personal favorite. The count moves quickly enough so that you'll be moving your bets up and down regularly. If you can be smooth about it, a 1 to 8 spread is not difficult to achieve. Coming off the top of the deck with a two or three unit bet about a third of the time may enable you to spread from 1 to 10. If you look for a decent cut card placement and don't play more than three-handed, that occasional two or three unit bet off the top won't be too big a factor.

The following table assumes average rules and normal deck penetration. Based on that, your *minimum* workable betting spread in each type of game is recommended. More is better if you can manage it.

NUMBER of DECKS	BETTING SPREAD
1	2/1/3
2	1 to 5
4	1 to 8
6	1 to 10

TABLE HOPPING

Another method of getting more money down as the favorite and less when the your a "dog" is leaving the table when the count goes substantially negative. At those times, your minimum bet would effectively be "zero".

An extension of this same principle is to approach a blackjack game in progress and count down the first few hands from the beginning of the deck/shoe. This is known as "backcounting". If the count climbs significantly into the "plus", jump in and play a bit. If not, move on towards the next table with the same game plan in mind.

Both techniques just described have been thoroughly outlined and advocated by two of the best practical blackjack authorities in the world; Arnold Snyder *(Blackbelt in Blackjack)* and Stanford Wong *(Professional Blackjack).* In fact, table hopping to the point where you play *only* when you have the count in your favor has actually been coined as "Wonging" in card counting jargon. These methods apply primarily to multiple deck play since there, the player is at a disadvantage about 80% of the time.

As a matter of general practice in shoe games, you should make it a point to quit for the day on a negative count rather than at the end of a shoe. The same goes for changing tables or breaking to eat. If you have reasons to remain at one specific table, you should relegate your bathroom breaks to periods where the count is seriously negative. You need to do whatever you can to minimize your percentage of time in action as the underdog. Once you've gone through the first 70 or 80 cards of a shoe and the count has been firmly entrenched on the negative side, there's no purpose in absorbing the ensuing cluster of disadvantageous deals. With six decks, this lasts a while!

149

Understand that with an unbalanced system like the Black Ace Count, you keep track of more low cards than high ones. This means that any time your running count is not *rising*, then more high cards have come out than low ones and your disadvantage has actually increased! *In fact, in a six deck game the shoe has become negative enough to bail out if your running count is "-5" (or worse) with the first deck gone; "+3" with two decks played out and "+8" with three decks in the discard tray (at those three checkpoints your count will be "10", "12" and "14" respectively when the shoe is merely "even").* But if you play past the first three decks, you might as well stay to see the next shoe.

The more precisioned Mentor Count *(from chapter 11)* is a different animal. *There, you'd pretty much like to jump ship if the "true count" reached -10 in the early going of a shoe or -7 midway through.* The table hopping guidelines below can help skew the overall distribution of cards you'll face somewhat more in your favor.

1) *Try to start off each playing session on a positive count via backcounting (enter @ +7 true w/ the Mentor Count or "20" w/ the Black Ace Count).*
2) *Change tables, visit the bathroom or take a break on serious negative counts.*
3) *Dedicate a partial segment of each play day to just "Wonging" it.*

PLAYING 2 HANDS

Many casual blackjack players routinely play two simultaneous hands. This of course all goes for naught since it will bring exactly the same results as two individual persons playing one hand apiece using identical strategies. Think about it. If seat *"A"* plays perfect basic strategy, he has a $1/2$% disadvantage in a multi-deck game. If seat *"B"*

150

plays the same way, he also has a $1/2$% disadvantage. If both seats just happen to be the same person, it makes no difference whatsoever!

But there are select occasions when a card counter can draw an advantage from playing two simultaneous hands! That's when the count is high and there are at least two other players at the table. As an example, let's say you're in a three-handed game and your count suggests a five unit bet. About 11 cards will be used up on each round. Of those 11 cards, you will get *one* hand. If you go to two hands, about 14 cards will be used for each *two* hands you're dealt. If there's about one deck left before the cut card comes out, you'll get in 5 hands playing them one at a time and 8 hands playing two at a time! *By playing two spots, you'll get down more hands in an advantageous situation!*

This however, is not quite as good as it sounds since both of your hands are played against the same dealer's hand. It's not really the same as playing two consecutive individual hands. For this reason, when playing two hands you should cut down the amount wagered on each to about 70% of what you'd play a single hand for. If your five unit bet would be $50 for one hand, two hands at $35 each would be an appropriate amount. That will adjust for the increased volatility of risking two bets against one dealer's hand, *but you'll get more total dollars in action as the favorite over the same number of cards dealt.* The more players there are at the table, the more there is to be gained by going to two hands with positive counts!

Also, on a "plus" count if it appears the last round is coming up, you should go to 2 or even 3 hands *regardless* of the number of players! You'll be sucking an extra hand or two out of the pack that you never would have gotten.

151

THE RIGHT TIME TO QUIT

It's an age-old question. When have you made enough money to lock up your winnings for the day, and when is it time to cut your losses and throw in the towel? This extremely prevalent question is generally looked at so illogically by people who are otherwise sensible and logical, yet it has such a simple answer. That's because determining if it's time to quit has nothing to do with whether you're winning or losing! An excellent example can be taken from the highly skillful game of poker.

Suppose you sat down at a casino poker table with a crew of total strangers. After an hour you realized you were playing with a table full of world class professionals. You were by far the weakest player, but you had made a couple of key hands and were winning. What should you do?

Since you'll almost certainly be beaten senseless if you continue to buck heads with them, you should definitely quit right now! And what if you were already losing? Same answer! Get out of there ASAP before they bleed you dry!

Now let's reverse it and say you've discovered you're playing with a bunch of complete suckers. You're head and shoulders above them all, but you've taken a few tough beats and are getting slaughtered! What should you do now?

Since you outclass the field, the "cream will eventually rise to the top" if you stick with it, so you should stay even though you're losing. And what if you were already winning? You're highly likely to keep right on winning, so again stay put!

Can you see that whether you should quit or keep gambling has nothing to do with how much you're winning or losing? Here are the sole determinants:

A) If you have the edge, you should always keep playing.
B) If you're the underdog, you should never have started, so quit right now!

Since it's impossible to accurately guess how fickle Lady

Luck will behave over the upcoming short term, your best estimate is always based upon *your odds to win from this point going forward.* If you're way behind and feel as though getting even is hopeless, then forget about getting even! Your only question should be, *"If I continue to play am I likely to win something starting right now?"* If you're still playing well and the game conditions are still right, your chance to pick up a few bucks *starting now* are just as good as they will be tomorrow or next week! Condition yourself to think this way and you'll see that it's true.

BANKROLLING

Just how much money do you need to be a blackjack card counter? Most of the better books have sophisticated formulas for determining this mathematically, and they are very accurate. But all you really need to be concerned with is, *"How much money do I need for the day, the week or the long haul to guard against going belly-up?"*

If you're headed to the casino for a three or four hour playing session, 60 of your *average* size bets will cover you the vast majority of the time. That means if you're spreading your bets from $15 to $200 and averaging about $30 per hand, $1800 *(60 x $30)* is a solid playing stake for the day.

If you'll be vacationing in Las Vegas for a week and think you might put in 25 or 30 hours at the blackjack tables, then 150 average bets should keep you in action throughout your trip. Betting $15 to $200, that would take $4500 of your hard earned money.

I once had the harrowing displeasure of enduring a negative swing lasting 150 hours that consumed nearly 400 average size bets. That's how much I think you need in your overall card counting bankroll to keep yourself afloat indefinitely. Below is a summary of your recommended bankrolling requirements as a blackjack card counter.

SESSION STAKE	60 average bets
VACATION STAKE	150 average bets
OVERALL BANKROLL	400 average bets

TABLE IMAGE

Once you find a not too crowded blackjack table with playable rules and decent penetration, you need to be able to sit down and receive the same deal as the average player without being subjected to anti-card-counting measures. The casinos know that fundamentally, blackjack can be beaten. They also know that not one gambler in a hundred, perhaps a thousand can play well enough to get the job done. But if they think you might be that one player, *you will draw heat!*

The floor people will begin to observe your play very closely. The cut card will probably be placed further from the bottom of the shoe, or deck. Some pit persons may actually count right along with you and have the dealer shuffle up when the deck goes positive, even if the cut card hasn't come out yet! They can tape you from the surveillance room and re-evaluate your play. You might have your picture taken from several angles and never be aware of it. The pit boss may drastically reduce the maximum betting limit at your table. And when you move to another table, the limit may be reduced there too, and brought back to normal at the table you just vacated. In the state of Nevada, they can flat out tell you to leave!

These are all things you must learn to avoid in order to not give up your edge. Playing unimpeded often requires a convincing "dumb act". You need to blend in with the

154

average sucker. That's what is meant by *"table image"*. When I play, I try not to appear very serious about what I'm doing. It helps to make a joke of it when you lose a big bet. ***And you will lose some big bets!***

:When I hit *16* against an *8* and bust with a *10*, I occasionally might show a little sportsmanship by jesting something like, *"Twenty-six so far; okay, hit me again!"*

:It can be good for your image if you appear to be drinking. Ice water in a cocktail glass with a squeeze of lime isn't a bad idea. Always try to seem loose and relaxed, as though you came to gamble it up.

:Sometimes, it's not a bad idea to ask for advice from the dealer or other players at the table on how they would play one of your close hands, then thank them if you win.

:When making an unusual but strategically astute play, you may need to express some shallow reason for doing it as a decoy. For example, when doubling down with *Ace/8* against a *6*, you might explain that you always soft double against a small card, ignoring the fact that you also have *19*.

:If the count goes positive at a table with at least three players and you want to "hog" more of those cards for yourself by playing two hands, you might say something like, *"Let's change the order of the cards and see if that helps"*.

:When I move to a new table and plop down my chips, often times the dealer or another player will ask, *"How's it going today?"* Sometimes I'll answer, *"Having one of my best days ever; only stuck $400!"*

:When you're not at third base and the other players have stayed pat with stiffs, if the dealer breaks you could mutter some nonsense about the third baseman having

155

"saved the table". It can also be good for your image if you "high-five" the player next to you every once in a while after the dealer breaks.

:It may be good to leave your chips in unruly piles suggesting that you are a disorganized sort. When I first sit down I spread my chips in a horizontal row flat on the table and leave them that way. Any chips I may win, I pile in front of those. Often times, somebody will ask me, "How did the craps table treat you?" Blackjack floorpeople like craps players.

:And if you really play well, you can occasionally afford to make an obvious, but slightly incorrect play when you're being watched, such as hitting with *13* against a *deuce*. If you hit that hand once for every eight times you're dealt it with a neutral count, it will take .001% off your overall game. But done in the right spot, it will make the kind of impression you want to make on your observers. Other low cost mistakes you can make for show are hitting *12* against a *4* or a *6* and standing with *16* against a *10* up.

One cautionary word about table image. Don't overdue it. Sometimes you can get carried away with your little act and bring attention to yourself that you never would have gotten playing it straight. If you manage your hands like you know exactly what you're doing, and act like a complete moron at the same time you may look more suspicious than anybody. But still, these are all things you should be able to do when the situation calls for it.

POISE

Be forewarned. Whether you have a 2% disadvantage as so many players do, or the 1% edge of a true expert you are *still gambling!* Some days you will labor through your whole act; phony drinks, silly jokes and all just to keep your welcome mat in place. And what will happen? ***You'll get your doors blown off as if you really are the sucker you were pretending to be!*** It will make you wonder what you were trying to protect in the first place. When things go wrong like this, ***poise*** is critical! The definition of *"poise"* in this context is: "Having the understanding and confidence that the way you're playing is right, and using the discipline to continue playing that way in the face of adversity".

Don't start lamenting to yourself, *"Poor me, I just can't win a hand; I double down to make 20 against a 5 and she pulls a six card 21 to beat me out of another hundred bucks! Un-effing-believable!"* Well, it's not unbelievable! It's is all part of this game!

When such events persist you'll be tempted to try something different; something that you know is not proper. Don't even think about it, because:

ANY TIME YOU DEPART FROM YOUR CORRECT STRATEGY IN AN EFFORT TO CHANGE THE RESULTS, YOU'RE MORE LIKELY TO CHANGE THEM FOR THE WORSE!

The best outcome, although it may be a disappointing one is most likely to be achieved by staying with the correct game plan. Remember, it's all one long gambling game landscaped with hills and valleys. You are on a continuous journey that will consume countless days and nights. Some nights you will park and rest on a hill, other nights in a valley. Only the altitude of your final destination is important. Staying on the prescribed course is more likely to get you where you want to go.

157

Multi-deck shoe games can be particularly discouraging. You may have hung close to even for an hour while patiently counting through neutral and negative shoes, then get unlucky and drop 30 units on the next few "high-count" hands! And what's the right move when the shuffle comes? *Go back into your shell, revert to a one unit bet and wait obediently for the next positive shoe!* If it doesn't come, it doesn't come! Don't break form whatever you do. Don't do something silly and give the edge back to the house. *Gambling is very unforgiving of undisciplined gamblers.*

You may suddenly find yourself $1000 behind and know that the methodical process of counting cards is unlikely to get you even today. But it's better to stick to your game and finish perhaps a $700 or $800 loser than to go on tilt and *invite disaster!* At times like these you'll be glad you kept your day job. Always remember:

NO MATTER HOW MUCH SCIENCE AND ART YOU MAY LEARN ABOUT BLACKJACK, IF YOU DON'T MAINTAIN POISE, YOU WILL NOT WIN!

If you're extremely disciplined, don't mind taking some terrible beatings along the way, and can do all these things accurately and convincingly, then you can *probably* net some extra spending cash from playing blackjack. But live the life of luxury consistently knocking down the big bucks? Highly unlikely! As I said before:

IT'S ONE TOUGH WAY TO MAKE SOME EASY MONEY!

Chapter 10
KEY POINTS

1) Gaining the upper hand at blackjack is a two step process; learning to beat the **game** and learning to beat the **house.**

2) All blackjack games are not "beatable". The rules, decks and dealing procedures are the contributing factors that can make a game "good" or "bad".

3) Of the three variables listed above, the most subtle is "dealing procedure".

4) "Deck penetration" can be worth more than $1/2\%$ in overall expectation to a card counter.

5) Crowded tables not only slow down your play, but also contribute to shallower overall effective penetration.

6) The betting spread a card counter needs in order to maintain an advantage escalates dramatically as the number of decks increases.

7) The card counter must establish a typical gambler's "table image" so as to avoid anti - card - counting countermeasures from the casino.

8) Without supreme discipline, fortitude and character, a card counter cannot succeed even though he may possess every other scientific and artful skill.

11

*the*Mentor Count

Now you're entering a level of blackjack strategy that is basically for devout blackjack aficionados. This is the world of fully structured, professional level card counting. If you're not rather obsessed with the game of casino "21", it's most likely not for you. But if you're truly exhilarated by the mental gymnastics of juggling numbers in your head to tell you how to bet your money and play your hands more efficiently, then by all means read on.

Nearly every card that is played out of the deck or shoe has an effect on your chances to win the following hand. The cards that help the dealer when they are still in the pack are the *2, 3, 4, 5, 6,* and *7*. The cards that help the player are the *9, 10, Jack, Queen, King* and *Ace*. The *8* is virtually meaningless. So in all, there are six dealer-helping cards and six player-helping cards.

In an effort to make your card count more thorough, you could try counting all the *2's* through *7's* as +1, and the

9's through *Aces* as -1. But that would lead to efficiency problems since some cards make much more difference than others as they are played out.

That's where the *multi-level* card count concept entered the picture. In the 1960's, Edward O. Thorp of *"Beat the Dealer"* fame developed his *"Ultimate Point Count"* for detecting with total accuracy where the betting advantage lies as cards are dealt out of play. Each card was counted with a plus or minus value in direct proportion to its own significance. For example, the most important card in the deck, the *five* was counted as +11. *Deuce*s were +5 and all the *tens* were -7. The other cards had their own assigned values as well. Thus, on the multi-level card count scale the Ultimate Point Count was regarded as a *"level eleven"* count system. It was 100% efficient, but practically 100% unusable.

But Thorp had a heck of a concept going. Since then, several other less radical multi-level card counting systems have been devised in an attempt to accurately monitor the ever-shifting percentages in blackjack. Two, three and four level systems were designed and marketed in the 1970's and '80's with claims of being devastatingly powerful in casino play.

However, hindsight once again proved to be the best judge. Subsequent computer programs were developed to test the performance of card counting systems, both simple and complex. They revealed that due to the natural law of diminishing returns it hardly pays to get super-sophisticated. A well-designed *single* level card count turned out to yield about 90% as much mathematical advantage as a well-designed level *four* system.

161

COMPARATIVE ANALYSIS of BLACKJACK COUNT SYSTEMS

I have run well over a billion computer simulated hands of blackjack with several assorted well known card counting systems to evaluate their comparative performances. The results of that analysis revealed the following advice:

IF YOU'RE REALLY SERIOUS ABOUT BLACKJACK AND WANT YOUR CARD COUNT TO YIELD THE MAXIMUM PRACTICAL EDGE, USE A GOOD LEVEL TWO SYSTEM.

The software used for running the count system analysis, *(as well as all other computer work in this book)* was *Stanford Wong's Blackjack Count Analyzer*. It recorded each count's overall performance, it's dollar earnings and the standard deviation *(luck factor)*. Each system was run for a total of 100 million hands. First, 50 million hands were played with two decks, then another 50 million with six decks. The rules were as follows:

> DEALER HITS SOFT 17
> DOUBLE ON ANY STARTING HAND
> DOUBLE AFTER SPLIT
> RE-SPLIT PAIRS TO 4 HANDS
> NO RE-SPLIT OF ACES
> NO SURRENDER

All hands were played "heads up". The cut card placement was at $1^1/2$ decks in shoe games with a 1 to 16 betting spread. In double deck play the last $3/4$ of a deck was cut off and a "2/1/10" spread was used. The results are printed on the next page.

162

COUNT SYSTEM	CARDS	2 DECK	6 DECK
Level 1 Systems	TRACKED	YIELD	YIELD
High-Low Count	10	1.08%	0.81%
Hi-Opt I	8	1.07%	0.78%
Green Fountain	12	1.10%	0.74%
Canfield Expert	10	1.03%	0.72%
Level 2 Systems			
Mentor Count	12	1.20%	0.89%
Zen Count	11	1.20%	0.87%
Hi-Opt II	10	1.15%	0.88%
Revere Point Count	11	1.18%	0.83%
Omega II	11	1.15%	0.81%
R&T Point Count	9	1.15%	0.80%
Level 3 Systems			
Wong Halves	12	1.19%	0.91%
Uston Advanced	12	1.18%	0.88%

Statistically, there is an 80% chance that each result is representative of its system's true ability within 0.03%. As you can see, there is not a great deal of difference between the performance of a good simple count and a good complex one. But there is *some* difference! Furthermore, notice that most of the increase in performance comes when you upgrade from level one to level two.

Of the count systems that appear above, about half keep track of the *Ace* within the count, and the other half ignore it. Each system was designed that way deliberately.

You see, with fully structured card counting systems there are two separate facets to their usefulness. The first is to determine when the player has an advantage on the next

163

hand due to the high/low strength of the cards that remain. This is called the system's *betting correlation*. The second facet indicates when it is better to play your hand contrary to the basic strategy, again because of the remaining cards. This is known as the count's *playing efficiency*. These two aspects of card counting are dealt with in greater detail in Peter Griffin's book, *"The Theory of Blackjack"*.

In designing a card count, when trying to optimize one characteristic, often the other has to be compromised. That's because the *Ace* is actually a "high-low" card, since sometimes it counts as *1* and sometimes as *11*. For that reason, counting the *Ace* along with the high cards is liable to mislead you in the play of your hand. A classic example would be when you're doubling down. If you have *9* or *10*, catching a high card, particularly an *Ace* is very desirable. But if you're doubling down with *11*, buying a *10* would be perfect but an *Ace* is the kiss of death! Hence, some experts believe the *Ace* should be ignored by the main count and perhaps kept track of separately.

Still, others insist that since the *Ace* is even more valuable than the *10* in determining when the player has the betting edge on the next hand, it mustn't be ignored but indeed counted as a "player-helping" high card.

Both arguments have merit. But overall, a card count's *betting* accuracy is more important than its *playing* accuracy. That's largely because strategic opportunities to increase your bet arise much more often than those occasions when you should "change-up" the play of your hand. The more decks you're playing with, the more this is so.

While analyzing the various count systems, my own curiosity on this controversial topic led me to experiment by fabricating new counts, first including then ignoring the *Ace*. Using Griffin's equations as design parameters, I derived level two and level three systems that included the *Ace* which yielded betting correlations of 98 to 99$^1/2$%. But their playing efficiencies were only in the mid-50's. By eliminating the *Ace*, I could achieve playing efficiencies in the high 60's, but their betting correlations then dropped into the low 90's. In the acid test of actual computer simulation runs, neither style outperformed the other perceptibly, nor any of the pre-existing count systems in that same class. But by manipulating the innards of these counts further, I finally struck on a level two arrangement that outperformed all other level two systems, and was on a par with the level three card counts. This, I affectionately dubbed, *the Mentor Count.*

The Mentor Count is a complete "level two" balanced count system with tables of index numbers that tell you when to vary your play from the basic strategy with roughly 80 different hands. It outperforms the majority of fully structured count systems on the public market today, *regardless of complexity.* Using it with an appropriate betting spread, you should improve your performance in the typical blackjack game by about 1$^1/2$% over the basic strategy. This count probably represents the practical upper limit for card counting systems *that do not employ a separate side-count of other cards.* It should be noted that counting systems which do not count the *Ace* probably have more to gain by keeping a separate side-count of *Aces* than those which already track the *Ace* within the count.

Most fully structured card counts have betting correlation ratings from 87% up to 99% no matter how simple or complicated they may be. Their playing

165

efficiencies range from about 50% up to 69%. The accuracy ratings of the Mentor Count are as follows:

Betting Correlation	**97%**
Playing Efficiency	**62%**

This superb mix makes the Mentor Count an excellent *"all-around-athlete"* for playing blackjack effectively against any number of decks without the added use of any side-counts. The Mentor Count is illustrated below:

The Mentor Count

CARD RANK

2	3	4	5	6	7	8	9	10	A
+1	+2	+2	+2	+2	+1	0	-1	-2	-1

Notice that the Mentor Count does include all the *Ace*s, but counts them with less impact than each of the *10's*. This was a key factor in achieving its high all-around performance. Incorporating the *deuce, 7* and *9* into the count with less value than the other more vital cards is also appropriate. Thus, the Mentor Count tracks virtually every card in the deck that matters *(the 8 does have minuscule value for playing the hand, but is nil for betting purposes)*.

BALANCED COUNTING

Notice that unlike the *Black Ace Count*, the Mentor system is a *balanced* card count. That is, all the small cards add up to +10 while the big cards total -10. This equality is

166

necessary in order to more accurately determine your betting advantage or disadvantage at *all* counts and when to take insurance. A balanced count is also needed for indicating when to make many "off-the-wall" plays like doubling down with *10* against a *10* or hitting *14* against a *deuce*.

When using any balanced system, you do not "pre-load" your initial count at the beginning of play with some positive number *(such as starting a six deck shoe with a count of "8")*. Instead, the nearly universal method is to begin at "even", or "zero" regardless of how many decks are used. As the small cards come out, you add 1 or 2 points to your count depending upon the card. With each big card that appears, subtract 1 or 2 points for each.

With the Mentor Count for example, starting at "zero", if the first card off the top of the pack was a *9*, your running count would move to -1. If the next six cards were;

your count would have gone from -1 to;

+1,   -1,   0,   +1,   -1,   -2

One of the trickiest things to do with a balanced count is to not mess up the running total when crossing back and forth from a positive to a negative count. As if that's not problematic enough, now the cocktail waitress may stop by and ask if you need a drink. It would be quite easy to inadvertently pick up the count at +2 instead of -2 at the start of the next hand.

A "100" COUNTING BASE

Because of that, I always begin my count off the top of a new pack at "100". When that *9* was the first card out, my running count would go to "99", *(meaning negative 1)*. Now, when those same next six cards were played, my count would run:

101, 99, 100, 101, 99, 98

I simply count forward and backward from 100. I never have to fool with "minuses" and there's no risk of accidentally changing signs between hands. This has been my method for nearly twenty years. I find it to be smoother and less error-prone. Just be aware that *a count of "92" really means "-8"!* In multi-deck play, the running count will sometimes get very far from "even". When this happens, you need to be comfortable with the idea that a count of "68" is actually "-32". But don't worry, even with six decks you will virtually never reach the ambiguous count of "50" in either direction.

After a short while, you'll feel comfortable dropping the *"hundred"* off a *"one-o-four"* count, and simply count "4, 3, 2, 1, 0, 99, 98, etc.". If you don't think this is easier, then stick to the conventional method of starting at "zero" and going into minus running counts. But either way, you must be able to count down a full single deck in 30 seconds maximum, or you're not ready.

the *TRUE* C*OUNT*

Another confusing aspect of full scale card counting systems is the necessity to convert the running count to the *"true count"*. Just what is the true count?

At the beginning of play with any number of full decks there are as many low cards *(2 through 7)* as high cards *(9 through Ace)*. When you get let's say, two decks into a six deck shoe, what would it mean if you had a running count of +10 *(or "110")?* Think about it. With the Mentor Count, *(since the six low ranks of cards add up to ten points)* it would mean that about six more *low* cards have come out than *high* cards. This in turn means there are six more *high* cards left in the shoe than *low* cards. With four decks of cards still remaining, that would put the theoretical total of available high cards at **99**, and the low cards at **93**.

But what if you still had a running count of +10 after five decks were gone? Now with only one deck left, the remaining supply of high to low cards should be **27** to **21**. In both cases there's a six card surplus of high ones. But in the first example, only $51^{1}/2\%$ of the remaining cards are high *(not counting the neutral 8's)*, and in the second case it's 56%! Considering that this ratio will hover around 50-50 during play, the second case is four times as extreme! In fact, a $51^{1}/2\%$ chance of catching a high card is no big deal, but 56% is! Yet in both cases the running count is +10.

BY CONSIDERING HOW MANY DECKS REMAIN, THEN ADJUSTING THE RUNNING COUNT APPROPRIATELY YOU GET WHAT'S KNOWN AS THE "TRUE COUNT".

169

The true count is what gives you an accurate indication of the *proportional* high/low strength of the remaining cards. That's the information you're really looking for.

How do you make this adjustment effectively? There are several ways. Most methods involve *division*, but I prefer to *multiply*. I always *calibrate*, or "true up" my running count to *two decks*. By that I mean, I want to bet my chips and play my hands as if there were two decks left. To do that, I multiply the running count by the *percentage* that two decks is, compared to the number of decks that actually remain. *Honestly, this is simpler than it sounds!*

For example in the first case above, two decks *(your constant reference point)* is *half* as much as the four remaining decks that you're actually playing from. So you multiply the running count of +10 by ¹/₂ to get a true count of +5. That's because a running count of +10 with four decks remaining will have the same percentage of high cards as a running count of +5 when two decks are left. You then go ahead and make your betting and playing decisions according to a true count of +5.

In the second case where there is only one deck left, two decks is *twice* as much as that lone remaining deck. So you multiply the running count of +10 by two to get a true count of +20. This is the right thing to do since the remaining cards in case number two are proportionally four times as rich in high cards as case number one.

By always using two decks as a "benchmark" you have a constant calibration point at which to evaluate the actual high/low strength of the running count.

It's easier for most folks to learn this concept in practical, down to earth terms. But technically speaking, the mathematical method for converting the running count to the true count can be expressed as follows:

$$\frac{2 \text{ DECKS}}{\text{\# of REMAINING DECKS}} \times \text{RUNNING COUNT} = \text{TRUE COUNT}$$

Performing this calculation at the tables can be unnerving. It's also unnecessary. All you really have to do is become familiar the chart shown below. It contains multipliers for converting the running count to the true count with just about any number of decks remaining.

TRUE COUNT CONVERSION CHART

REMAINING DECKS	MULTIPLIER
6	$1/3$
5	.4
4	.5
$3^1/_2$	.6
3	$2/3$
$2^1/_2$	.8
2	1
$1^1/_2$	$1^1/_3$
$1^1/_3$	$1^1/_2$
1	2
$2/3$	3
$1/_2$	4
$1/_3$	6

It makes no difference how many decks you started with. All that matters is the running count and the number of cards that are left. The running count **x** the multiplier for the remaining decks will give you the true count, which is a literal indicator of the high/low strength of the pack you're currently playing from. Let's run through a few examples together:

Five decks left; running count is +10.
.4 x +10 = +4 true count

Three decks left; running count is -18
$2/3$ of -18 = -12 true count

Two decks left; running count is +13
with 2 decks left, the R/C always = the T/C

Two-thirds of a deck left; running count is +9
3 x +9 = +27 true count

After you've converted a few running counts into their true counts, you'll see that most of your advantageous betting situations will occur late in the deck or shoe. That's why good penetration is so important. And overall, the fewer decks that are used, the better.

Remember, as cards are coming out you apply them to your *running count*. Then you must keep that running count in the back of your mind while you convert to the *true count* to size your bet or play your hand. After you've done that, pick up the running count again and update it as cards come into play.

How will you know how many decks are left? The discard rack is your source of information. You'll need to become an astute judge of how many cards are in a given

172

stack. Two decks of cards stand about $1^1/8$ inches tall. That's equal to a stack of nine chips. During play, whatever is in the discard rack plus a bit more for the cards on the board will leave the remainder in the shoe. A little practice at home will teach you to gauge the remaining cards reasonably well.

CAUTION! *Be careful about deviating from the basic strategy after you've converted to the true count! Realize that you're always **estimating** how many decks remain, plus your multiplication may be less than perfect.* Because of this I like to see the true count exceed the index number *(shown later)* for that particular hand by 10 or 15% before I "change up" my play. In that way I don't run the risk of playing worse than a basic strategy player. Sizing your bet is not as sensitive. Either you'll have an edge or you won't. It's not as big a deal if you mistakenly bet 4 units when you really should have only bet 3. You had the advantage either way. The most important part of sizing your bet according to the true count is making sure you indeed have an edge before you increase your bet. When you're not positive, sometimes a two unit wager is a good idea. That will either be mathematically appropriate, or good for table image purposes.

BETTING and PLAYING STRATEGY
for the
MENTOR COUNT

This is the heart of the Mentor Count system; betting your money and playing your hands. With any card count you generally want to start betting multiple units when the count has risen high enough to erase your handicap and give you an advantage of about $1/2$%. In an average game *(-.4 to -.5% basic strategy disadvantage)*, this occurs at a true count of about +7 with the Mentor system. Each point in true count will change your advantage by about $1/8$%. Use the "rules variations" table from Chapter 5 to adjust your betting schedule in uncommon rules/decks.

The *hypothetical* betting schedule outlined below is for average quality blackjack games with any number of decks. It describes how you would love to spread your bets if there were no restrictions put on your play at all.

TRUE COUNT	BET SIZE
+5 or lower	1 unit
+6	2 units
+7	3 units
+9	4 units
+11	6 units
+13	10 units
+15 or higher	15 units

This is what you should come to recognize as being *strategically ideal*. Now what about the *real world?* In single deck play you may have to forget about going beyond 3 units, so stick with a 3 unit wager at +7 or higher. With double decks, 6 units at +11 or higher may be your cap. This is where the art comes into your play. With a four deck shoe, 10 units at +13 or greater will probably work. With six decks, 15 units shouldn't be a problem if you're smooth about it.

174

VARIABLE STRATEGY
INDEX NUMBERS

With the Black Ace Count there were just nine hands that you would play differently from the basic strategy when your running count reached "20". What you didn't concern yourself with, was the fact that there were also several other hands that should have been played differently when the count climbed *beyond* that.

You see, the Black Ace Count was calibrated to evaluate your advantage efficiently when the running count was "20" with any number of cards remaining. But beyond "20", it was inaccurate. If you had a running count of "24" for example, you knew you had a bigger advantage than at "20". But how much more always depended upon the number of cards that were left. Thus, at very high counts, you knew it was appropriate to bet a lot of money. But you could never be sure that your count was high enough to cause you to play some additional hands differently.

With the true count feature used in the Mentor system, you'll have an effective indicator of your advantage *(or handicap)* across the entire range of counts that you will be exposed to. With the true count you'll be aware of some rare times that it will be best to double down with *8* against a *4*, hit *14* against a *4* and even split a pair of *10's* against a *4!*

Following is your master strategy chart for the Mentor Count. Each index number within the boxes indicates the *true count* at which it becomes better to play that particular hand *differently* from the basic strategy. If the box is shaded, then *always* play that hand *according* to the basic strategy.

175

HIT / STAND TABLE

IF THE TRUE COUNT IS EQUAL TO, OR MORE POSITIVE
THAN THE INDEX NUMBER, STAND: OTHERWISE HIT.
(Use Basic Strategy for all shaded squares)

DEALER'S UP-CARD

HAND	2	3	4	5	6	7	8	9	10	A
12	13	7	0	-7	-4*					
13	-2	-6	-11	-17	-17					
14	-12	-15	-20							
15								30	15	
16								22	1	30*
17										

*IF DEALER HITS SOFT 17, THEN: 12 vs. 6 is: -12, and 16 vs. ACE is: +15.

Look at the box that corresponds with *12* against a dealer's *2* up. The index number is 13. The basic strategy says to hit *12* against a *deuce*. But if the true count is +13 or more positive, it would be better to stand with this hand. Now look at *14* against a *4*. Notice that its index number is -20. If the true count is more negative than -20, you should take a card rather than stand. Throughout the "HIT/STAND" table, if the true count is more negative than the index number you should hit. If it is equal to or more positive than the number, you should stand. In any shaded squares, you will always follow the basic strategy.

Notice also, that some of the index numbers are very small, such as with *12* against a *4*, or *16* against a *10* up. These are hands that you will be changing your play with quite often. When playing your hands by the true count, forget about more preliminary rules such as hand composition or board composition. The true count supersedes everything.

176

DOUBLE DOWN TABLE

IF THE TRUE COUNT IS EQUAL TO, OR MORE POSITIVE
THAN THE INDEX NUMBER, DOUBLE DOWN: OTHERWISE HIT.
(Use Basic Strategy for all shaded squares)

DEALER'S UP-CARD

HAND	2	3	4	5	6	7	8	9	10	A
8			21	13	7					
9	3	-3	-9	-16		12	30			
10						-17	-7	15	15	
11								-18	-15	3*

* IF DEALER HITS SOFT 17, THEN, 11 vs. ACE is: -2

To use an example from the double down table, double with *9* against a *7* up if the true count is +12 or more positive, otherwise follow the basic strategy and hit. Also notice that there is occasionally an asterisk (*) in an index box. These are hands that are affected by the dealer's *"soft 17"* rule. The number inside the box pertains to the dealer standing on *soft 17*. If the dealer hits a *soft 17*, the number that replaces it is given at the bottom of the table.

SOFT DOUBLING TABLE

IF THE TRUE COUNT IS EQUAL TO, OR MORE POSITIVE
THAN THE INDEX NUMBER, DOUBLE DOWN.
(Use Basic Strategy for all shaded squares)

DEALER'S UP-CARD

HAND	2	3	4	5	6	7	8	9	10	A
A/2			12	0	-8					
A/3			7	-10						
A/4			-2	-18						
A/5		10	-7							
A/6	4	-10	-20							HIT / STD
A/7	3	-6	-18							3*
A/8		19	11	5	3*					
A/9			22	18	17					

* IF DEALER HITS SOFT 17, then A/8 vs. 6 is: -1 and ALWAYS HIT A/7 vs. A

Out at the lower right hand area of the soft doubling table, the "3*" in the box pertains to *hitting* and *standing* with *Ace/7* vs. an *Ace*, rather than doubling down. If the dealer stands on *soft 17*, hit unless the true count is +3 or greater, then stand. But if the dealer hits on *soft 17*, then *always* hit this hand.

PAIR SPLITTING

(WITHOUT "DOUBLE AFTER SPLIT")

IF THE TRUE COUNT IS EQUAL TO, OR MORE
POSITIVE THAN THE INDEX NUMBER, SPLIT.

(Use Basic Strategy for all shaded squares)

DEALER'S UP-CARD

HAND	2	3	4	5	6	7	8	9	10	A
2/2	25	9	-2	-14						
3/3		12	-3	-14						
4/4										
6/6	6	-5	-12	-20						
7/7										
8/8									(25)	
9/9	-4	-9	-13	-20	-20	30				24
10/10		30	22	18	17					
A/A										-20

(25) - USE IN REVERSE: IF TRUE COUNT EXCEEDS +25, DON'T SPLIT

One hand in the pair splitting table is acted upon in reverse. With a pair of *8's* against a *10* up, keep splitting *until* the true count rises to +25, then stand.

Also, as you might intuitively guess, when the true count is too negative to split, some pairs should be hit while others should be stood with. For that, follow the "hit/stand" table. A rare example is a pair of *6's* against a *4* up. If the true count were, let's say -15, you should no longer split; but you should also no longer stand since the index number for *12* against a *4* is "0"! Usually however, when a hand should no longer be split, the basic strategy should be followed.

178

PAIR SPLITTING
(WITH "DOUBLE AFTER SPLIT")
IF THE TRUE COUNT IS EQUAL TO, OR MORE
POSITIVE THAN THE INDEX NUMBER, SPLIT.
(Use Basic Strategy for all shaded squares)

DEALER'S UP-CARD

HAND	2	3	4	5	6	7	8	9	10	A
2/2	-12	-17								
3/3	-3									
4/4		30	12	-2	-7					
6/6	-6	-13	-20							
7/7							15			
8/8								(25)		
9/9	-10	-15	-19			18				18
10/10		30	22	18	17					
A/A										-20

(25) - USE IN REVERSE: IF TRUE COUNT EXCEEDS +25, DON'T SPLIT

When you can double down after splits, not only are there more pairs that should in fact be split, but the margin by which you should split many pairs becomes greater. That's because you might catch a card that will give you a good doubling hand, which makes splitting even more advantageous than it was before.

179

SURRENDER

IF THE TRUE COUNT IS EQUAL TO OR MORE
POSITIVE THAN THE INDEX NUMBER, SURRENDER
(Use Basic Strategy for all shaded squares)

DEALER'S UP-CARD

HAND	8	9	10	A	A
				STAND SOFT 17	HIT SOFT 17
13			27		
14		20	10	17	10
15	28	9	-1	6	-2
16	18	0	-10	-6	-20
17					(7)
8/8		30	8		*

(7) - USE IN REVERSE: SURRENDER UP TO +7,
THEN STAND.
*WITH 1 OR 2 DECKS ALWAYS SPLIT: WITH 4 TO
8 DECKS ALWAYS SURRENDER.

The surrender option is significantly affected by the *soft 17* rule. When the dealer has an *Ace* up, one thirteenth of the time he'll turn up a *6* from underneath making a *soft 17*. Consequently, there are two separate columns for when to surrender against an *Ace* showing.

INSURANCE: Take insurance whenever the true count is **+9** or more positive in single deck play, **+11** in double deck games, and **+12** when using four or six decks.

On the following page is a condensed pocket size edition of the *Mentor Variable Playing Strategy*. Photocopy it, laminate it and carry it with you.

180

	2	3	4	5	6	7	8	9	10	A
8			21	13	7					
9	3	-3	-9	-16		12	30			
10							-17	-7	15	15
11								-18	-15	3*
12	13	7	0	-7	-4*					
13	-2	-6	-11	-17	-17					
14	-12	-15	-20							
15								30	15	
16								22	1	30*
17										
A/2			12	0	-8					
A/3			7	-10						
A/4			-2	-18						
A/5		10	-7							
A/6	4	-10	-20							
A/7	3	-6	-18							3*
A/8		19	11	5	3*					
A/9			22	18	17					
2/2	25	9	-2	-14						
3/3		12	-3	-14						
4/4										
6/6	6	-5	-12	-20						
7/7										
8/8									(25)	
9/9	-4	-9	-13	-20	-20	30				24
10/10		30	22	18	17					
A/A										-20

surrender

14	20	10	17
15	9	-1	6
16	0	-10	-6

The VALUE of a
VARIABLE PLAYING STRATEGY

Lots of card counters have learned how to keep track of the cards and bet their money according to the true count. However, not all that many go to the lengths of memorizing scores of index numbers for how to play their hands. Many just play all their hands according to the basic strategy regardless of the count. It's already been mentioned that *betting* by the count is more important than *playing* by the count. But how much more important? That depends upon the number of decks.

181

Following are the results of a computer simulation run using the Mentor Count in our model two deck game *(hit soft 17 w/dbl. aft. spl.)*. Player performances are listed for 4 different modes of play.

A) Basic Strategy with flat bets   -.44%
B) Mentor Variable Strategy with flat bets   -.14%
C) Mentor Count for betting w/ basic strategy   +.87%
D) Mentor Count for betting and playing   +1.20%

With two decks, it appeared that betting by the count was about four times as useful as playing by the count. Further experimentation revealed that in round numbers, playing by the count and making flat bets will outperform the basic strategy by the following amounts.

w/ SINGLE DECK   .5%
w/ TWO DECKS   .3%
w/ FOUR DECKS   .2%
w/ SIX DECKS   .15%

In the *Mentor Count* you have one of the most potent card counting systems available for the human mind. Combining that with the "table savvy" traits mentioned in Chapter 10, you will be fully equipped to take on the casino at their own game, on their court and gain the upper hand. The only ingredient *you* must add is your own personal implementation. You'll need to become that *scholar/hustler* spoken of on the previous pages of this book. That's the part that stops *most* players; *will it stop you?*

182

Chapter 11
KEY POINTS

1) There are over a dozen different "fully structured" card counting systems in use today. Some track only eight ranks of cards with a value of +/-1 point each, while others count twelve ranks with a value of +/- 1 through 4 points each.

2) There is not a great deal of difference between the performances of a well designed single level count and a well designed level 4 count.

3) Most of any improvement from adding "levels" to a card count comes when upgrading from level 1 to level 2.

4) The Mentor Count is a top performing level 2 system that is on a par with most level 3 and level 4 systems.

5) The Mentor Count requires converting to the true count for betting and playing the hand.   A "quick-conversion" chart is enclosed to ease the process.

6) The Variable Playing Strategy charts contain about 80 index numbers to indicate when specific hands should be played differently from the basic strategy.

7) Playing a complete variable playing strategy will improve a card counter's overall performance by roughly .15% to .50% depending upon the number of decks used.

183

RECOMMENDED READING

I have read many blackjack books in my day. I feel that some of them paint too rosy a picture and make winning sound automatic as long as you learn to count. Others are more realistic, instructional and helpful. On the next two pages is a list of the more "up-to-date" books I've read that I feel give an educational and accurate representation of what playing blackjack to win the casino's money is like. Much of what I have learned about the game of *"21"* has been gleaned from these books.

Blackbelt in Blackjack by Arnold Snyder, RGE publishing
Originally written in the early '80's then redone in 1998, this "hands on" down to earth manual provides some of the best coverage of blackjack basics and advanced skills to be found anywhere. It contains a visually graphic definition of the "true count" concept and a detailed 30 page chapter on shuffle tracking. Three count systems; Red-7, Hi-Lo Lite and the excellent Zen Count are featured.

Professional Blackjack by Stanford Wong, Pi Yee Press
Very strong in the technical aspects of the game, Wong provides correct strategies and player's expectations for virtually all rule and deck variations. Monster charts supply the percentages for every player's hand vs. dealer's up-card. Two pro-level card counts; the Hi-Lo and Halves are included in ultra-fine detail.

Theory of Blackjack by Peter Griffin, Huntington Press
Griffin supplies gobs of math-based blackjack theory. From his conceptual analyses are derived definitive evaluations of card count betting and playing effectiveness, relative costs of misplaying hands and extremely precise basic strategy packages for different rules/decks.

184

Playing Blackjack as a Business by Lawrence Revere, *Lyle Stuart Publishing.* Hailing from the early 70's, it has become a "bible" for *"21"* players. Printed with many multi-colored charts, it's extremely clear though it focuses primarily on single deck play.

Blackjack Essays by Mason Malmuth, 2+2 Publishing
Malmuth is a highly descriptive writer. For the ongoing blackjack player he analyzes scores of controversial blackjack topics in a clear and unbiased manner. Good for building your sense of direction.

Blackjack Attack by Don Schlesinger, RGE publishing
A terrific collection of truly important card counting situational considerations analyzed and quantified exquisitely by the author. Contains a gold mine of information.

190 Million Hands of Blackjack by Bill Brown, *Casinos Plus.* For the statistical minded player. Shows how many times you win and lose each hand depending upon how it's played. Comes in $8^{1}/_{2}$ x 11, spiral bound.

Best Blackjack by Frank Scoblete, *Bonus Books*
A "soup to nuts" coverage of the game in general depth from basic strategy to card counting to playing for comps. Printed in 1996; a good overview of modern day blackjack.

Blackjack for Blood by Bryce Carlson, *CompuStar Press*
A thorough operational handbook for the card counter. Includes many pro-level "tricks of the trade". Built around the *Omega II*, an excellent single deck count.

Blackjack; take the Money & Run by Henry Tamburin, *Research Services Unlimited.* For the average casino goer, provides a well-rounded instructional approach to effective blackjack play.

Glossary of Blackjack Terms

Ace Side-count - keeping a separate track of the Aces that are played.
Anchor Seat - "3rd base"; last to act before the dealer.
Backcount - tracking the cards while observing a game in progress.
Balanced Count - count systems whose high + low cards total to zero.
Barring - permanently ejecting a player, often for counting cards.
Basic Strategy -optimum strategy without regard for the played cards.
Betting Spread - the ratio between a player's min. & max. bet.
Betting Correlation - a card count's ability to track the betting edge.
Borderline Hand - one in which the correct decision is very marginal.
Break the deck -shuffling prematurely, usually to thwart card counting.
Card Counting - keeping track of the cards that have been played.
Even Money - taking insurance when you have blackjack.
First Base - the seat to the dealer's immediate left and first to act.
Flat Bet - betting the same amount on every hand.
Hard Hand - a hand containing an Ace counted as "1", or no Ace at all.
Head Up - playing alone against the dealer.
Heavy Board - an excess of 10-count cards on the board.
House Edge - mathematical advantage the casino has over the player.
Index Number -true count at which it becomes advantageous to play a
hand differently from the basic strategy.
Insurance - betting that the dealer has a 10-card underneath her Ace.
Light Board - a deficiency of 10-count cards on the board.
Mimic the Dealer - to play all your hands the same as the dealer.
Natural - a blackjack; "21" on the first two cards.
Never Bust Strategy - to never risk hitting a stiff hand (12 through16).
Paint - any picture card such as a Jack, Queen or King.
Pat - to stand and take no more cards.
Penetration - how far the deck is dealt out before the shuffle.
Playing Efficiency - a card count's accuracy at detecting when the
basic strategy should be deviated from.
Progressive Betting - sizing your next bet according to the last result.
Push - a "tie", such as when both player and dealer have "18".
Running Count - an up-to-date tally of high vs. low played cards.
Shuffle Track - monitoring points in the pack where valuable cards lie.
Snapper - slang for a dealt blackjack.
Soft Hand - a hand containing an Ace counted as "11".
Stiff - a hard hand between 12 and 16 (inclusively).
Third Base - seat to the dealer's immediate right and last to act.
Toke - a tip for a dealer or cocktail waitress.
True Count - gauging the high-low ratio of the unplayed cards.
Unit - the minimum wager in a player's betting spread.

INDEX

A

Ace side-count - 163
Advantage Strategy - 125, 133

B

backcounting - 149, 150
balanced counting - 122, 166
bankroll - 154
basic principle of
    profitable gambling - 13, 15,
    17, 18, 22, 81, 128
basic strategy - 62, 66, 67, 68,
"Beat the Dealer" - 10, 161
betting correlation - 164
betting spread - 146
betting progressions - 50, 51
Black Ace Count - 131, 132, 175
Blackjack Count Analyzer - 162
blackjack myths - 35
blackjack's primary
    fundamentals - 63, 64
borderline hands - 94
board-sensitive hands - 97,
        99, 103
built-up hands - 107
bust-out rate, dealer's - 70

C

Canfield Expert System - 163
Caribbean Stud - 16, 65
collision insurance - 22
commonly misplayed hands - 72
composition sensitive
    hands - 95
counting at base "100" - 168
counting process - 119
count systems analysis - 163

D

dealer's bust card - 49
deck cutoff - 141, 142
deck penetration - 141
dependent events - 17
double down - 27
doubling for less - 88
dream blackjack - 87
dumb act - 154

E

ESP - 57
evening out process - 38
eye in the sky - 26

G

glossary - 186
Green Fountain Count - 163
Griffin, Peter - 164

H

hand odds (player's) - 90
heat - 154
heavy board - 100
hierarchy of play - 101
Hi-Lo Count - 163
Hi-Opt I Count - 163
Hi-Opt II Count - 163
hit/stand - 27
100 counting base - 168

I

independent events - 13, 18
insurance - 29, 31, 81, 83, 127
insuring a good hand - 82
intermediate card count - 132
index numbers - 175

187

K

Key Card Count - 118

L

layout, blackjack - 25
Let It Ride - 16
light board - 100
loophole in blackjack - 116
lop-sided results - 38

M

maximizing player options - 21
Mentor Count - 166
minimum betting spread - 148
money management - 50
multi-level card counts - 161

N

no mid-shoe entry - 45, 46
number of players - 143

O

Omega II Count - 163

P

pinochle blackjack - 110
pitch game - 25
playable rules - 140
playing efficiency - 164
progressive betting - 50
"Professional Blackjack" - 45
practice counting - 122

R

recommended reading - 184
replacement - 12
Revere Point Count - 163
R & T Point Count - 163
roulette - 12, 19
rule variations - 87
running count - 119, 123

S

"sacred" order of cards - 44
session stake - 154
shuffle-ups - 147
shorthanded play - 144
soft doubles - 78
soft hands - 78
soft 17 - pg 27
Spanish 21 - pg110
split pairs - 28, 67
starting hand - 94
streaks - 52, 57
"strip-blackjack" - 112
"sucker blackjack" - 87
surrender - 32, 69
switches - 56

T

table image - 149
"Theory of Blackjack" - 164
Thorp, Edward O. - 10, 161
true count - 123, 164
true count conversion - 171

U

unbalanced counting - 123
Ultimate Point Count - 161
Up-Graded Blk. Ace Ct. - 135
Uston Advanced Pt. Ct. - 163

V

vacation stake - 154
variable playing strategy - 181

W

Wong, Stanford - 45
Wong Halves Count - 163
"Wonging" - 149, 150

Z

Zen Count - 163